ISBN: 9781314545166

Published by:
HardPress Publishing
8345 NW 66TH ST #2561
MIAMI FL 33166-2626

Email: info@hardpress.net
Web: http://www.hardpress.net

REV. J. LOFTHOUSE IN ESKIMO COSTUME.

A THOUSAND MILES FROM A POST OFFICE

Or, TWENTY YEARS' LIFE AND TRAVEL
IN THE HUDSON'S BAY REGIONS

BY THE RIGHT REV.

J. LOFTHOUSE, D.D.

(LATE) BISHOP OF KEEWATIN

WITH A PREFACE BY THE

ARCHBISHOP OF CANTERBURY

WITH ILLUSTRATIONS

TORONTO

THE MACMILLAN COMPANY OF CANADA

AT ST. MARTIN'S HOUSE

1922

PREFACE

I DO not envy the men who find this little book uninteresting. The simple facts, simply told, of experiences such as these give to the dullest of us food for thought. What we call civilization makes life easy for us in the quiet round of home experience, and it is wholesome as well as stimulating to be thus reminded by a devoted servant of our Lord of the struggles nobly made, year in and year out, by a pioneer who is facing the hardships of the frozen North. We thank God that we have such a one among us to tell us thus simply of the kind of life which the Christian Missionary in those regions has to live " in journeyings often, in perils of waters, in perils in the wilderness, in weariness and painfulness, in watchings often," and, very markedly, in hunger and thirst and cold. No one can read the book without feeling how the writer loved his life-work for all its trials. It is because he thus loved it that others were brought to love the Master whom he serves so well.

RANDALL CANTUAR.

LAMBETH PALACE,
    19 *July*, 1922.

iii

CONTENTS

v

vi Contents

LIST OF ILLUSTRATIONS

vii

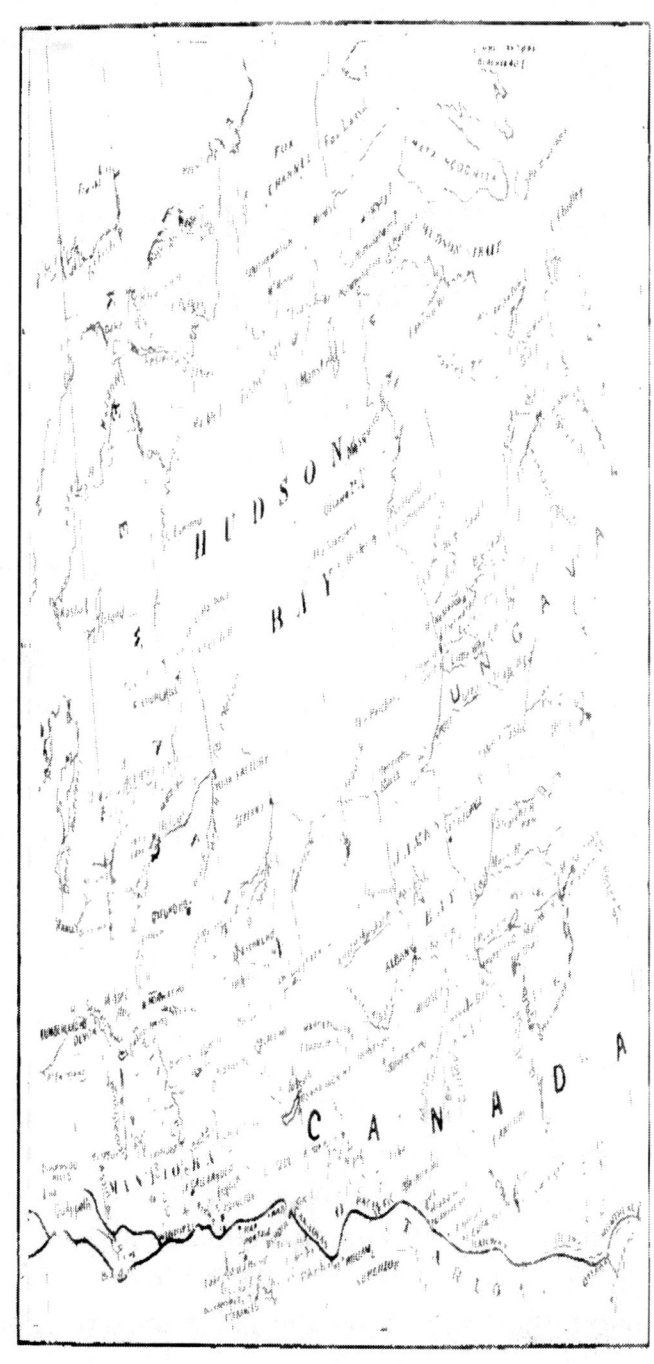

A THOUSAND MILES FROM A POST OFFICE

CHAPTER I

THE START FOR HUDSON'S BAY
(1882)

In the year 1882 a party of missionaries was organized by the Church Missionary Society, under the charge of the Rev. James Hannington, afterwards first Bishop of Equatorial Africa, volunteers being asked for from the students of the Church Missionary College. Amongst others, my name was sent in together with that of a dear friend and fellow-student, but neither of us was accepted, and we were prevented from laying down our lives for Africa, as most of that party afterwards did, though my fellow-student died in South Africa after working for some years as a missionary in China.

Very much to my surprise, a few weeks later, I was asked by the Committee of the Society to go to a very different part of the world and join Bishop Horden, the first Bishop of Moosonee in Hudson's Bay, with the object of establishing a Mission amongst the Eskimos on the north-western shores

of that vast inland sea, so well called the " Mediter-
ranean of Canada."

The word Bay can easily be seen to be somewhat
of a misnomer when it is once realized that you could
put the whole of the British Isles into the " Bay "
and then sail right round them without sighting
land anywhere. Hudson's Bay is nearly sixteen
hundred miles long and over six hundred miles
broad at its widest part.

My own knowledge of the Bay, or for that matter
of Canada itself, was at that time of the vaguest—
the average Englishman's hazy idea of the Colonies—
but I most willingly accepted the offer, and in a few
weeks had completed all preparations for the long
and trying journey to a strange and unknown
country.

At that time there was practically only one way
of reaching the Bay and that was by the annual
ship of the Hudson's Bay Company, which visited
the trading posts and mission stations, taking in
supplies and bringing back the lovely and valuable
furs caught the previous winter by the Indians,
for there is no fur-hunting done in the summer.

We sailed from London in June in the schooner
Prince of Wales, a good stout sailing vessel of some
five hundred tons, with a crew of twenty all told.
It would hardly bear comparison either as regards
comfort or accommodation with an ocean liner or
with some of the vessels now running into the Bay,
but this did not trouble me much at the time.

The Start for Hudson's Bay

Captain Bishop, an old and tried servant of the Hudson's Bay Company, was in charge. He was a typical sea dog of those days. No man living was his superior in the art of ice navigation. He had been through Hudson's Strait and Bay dozens of times and had always come through unscathed.

To leave home for the first time for an unknown country is not one of the easiest things, but it is a comfort in this, as in other things, to have a companion in tribulation, and a fellow-missionary, the Rev. H. Nevitt, was going out to work amongst the Indians at Moose Factory.

We dropped gently down the Thames in bright fine weather, but alas! it did not last long, for hardly had the pilot left us before we were struck by a very severe gale, and both Nevitt and I soon found out what it was to be at sea for the first time. For ten days we were tossed about like a cork, driven backwards and forwards, but making little headway. What a time it was! Driven right along the coast of Norway, we had several very narrow escapes, but at last made our way through the Pentland Firth and came safely to anchor in the beautiful land-locked inner harbour of Stromness in the Orkney Isles.

Both of us were very glad to get ashore. After a day or two of squeamishness I got my sea legs and also a sea appetite, but my poor friend remained in his berth all the time with little or no desire for the greasy soup and salt junk which formed our staple food.

3

A Thousand Miles from a Post Office

A ten days' sojourn in the Orkneys gave us some idea of the life and customs of the people, who were most kind and hospitable. We wandered all over the island, and visited the quaint old cathedral and palace of Kirkwall.

Meanwhile our ship was taking in supplies for her long journey across the Northern Atlantic, but had to wait some days for her consort or sister ship going to York Factory on the western side of the Bay.

Leaving Stromness on the 1st of July, we passed through the Hoy Sound with the " Old Man of Hoy " towering on our left, and soon found ourselves in the long rolling swell of the Northern Atlantic, but now we were able fully to enjoy the life at sea—soup and all.

After passing Cape Farewell, the southern point of Greenland, we reached Hudson's Strait. Here we got our first sight of ice—in fact, nothing but ice was in sight. There were almost numberless icebergs, every one of which seemed to dwarf the topmast of our ship, making the masts look like " little sticks." No ordinary ocean-going vessel could possibly have withstood the continual grinding and crushing. A matchbox under the foot of a man would have as much chance of resisting the mighty pressure. But the *Prince of Wales* was doubly sheathed with the stoutest oak, and thrust her way into the ice with little or no fear of being crushed.

For three weeks we were fast in the ice; being dependent on the wind, we were only able to use any

4

little " lead " that might open out. We were truly thankful when at last, by a good deal of tacking and beating about, we were able to make our way through the Strait. After reaching the Bay an incident happened which might have been very serious but for the careful watchfulness of our captain. Running along under a steady, stiff breeze, we sighted an immense berg some distance off but bearing steadily down upon us. The captain was below, the chief mate on deck. He seemed quite sure we would weather the berg, and kept steadily on his course whilst we stood gazing upon its vast proportions. When the captain quietly walked on deck, he looked round, saw the berg, and in a thundering voice cried, " 'Bout ship." Most of the sailors were below, it being the dog watch, but in a moment they all came tumbling up, many of them in very undress uniform, and hauling with a ready will they got the ship round and we stood away from the dangerous suction which might very easily have drawn us right on to the berg. The mate thought the " old man " had made a mistake. It may have been so, but I could not help feeling that it was wiser to be safe than sorry.

The voyage down the Bay was void of any incident beyond seeing a whale or two and a large number of porpoise, or white whales. About the middle of August we came in sight of a beacon at the mouth of the Moose River, and soon after picked up the land which was to be my home for so many years.

A Thousand Miles from a Post Office

Moose Fort, or Factory as it is often called, was then, and is still, the chief trading post of the southern part of Hudson's Bay. It stands on an island in the Moose River, and is some fifteen miles from the sea. It is a lovely spot and very attractive, or at least appeared so to us in the month of August after a long and tedious voyage of two months. It is a very different place in the long cold winter.

Here, thirty-one years before our arrival, John Horden, an Exeter man, had begun his noble work amongst the Cree Indians. He laboured amongst them until, ten years later, he laid down his life in their midst, stoutly refusing to give up his work and retire to England.

We were met and given a most hearty welcome by the Ven. Archdeacon Vincent, then in charge of the Mission (Bishop Horden, who was travelling from England by way of Canada, not having yet reached Moose), and by the Rev. E. J. Peck, the first missionary of the Church of England to the Eskimos of Hudson's Bay. Mr. Peck had travelled 500 miles in a very small boat in order to meet me, as I was to get my first insight into Eskimo life and work under him at Little Whale River on the eastern side of the Bay.

The distance between Moose Fort and this mission station is about five hundred miles around the shores of the Bay; this was to be covered in a small birch-bark canoe with a full month's provision, bedding, etc., for ourselves, three men, and a boy. I very soon discovered that missionaries in Hudson's Bay did not hamper themselves with an over-abundant supply of either luggage or food. Our outfit consisted of a blanket for each person, flour, fat bacon, tea, and sugar.

Our troubles began before we had gone 5 miles. The canoe was old and leaky, and soon I found myself sitting in some inches of water, so we landed for the night in order to patch her up. The prospect of travelling over 500 miles along a rough sea-coast during the month of September, with winter already coming on, in such a craft was by no means reassuring to a " tenderfoot," but there was no other way out, so we resolved to push on and take our chance. Next day we made our way down to the mouth of the river, where the *Prince of Wales* was at anchor.

At night we landed on a mud-flat, inhabited solely by mosquitoes. It was my first introduction to these pests of the north, but they at once waived all rules of etiquette and welcomed me with most enthusiastic affection. They invaded our tent, entirely against our strongly expressed wishes; do what we would there was no keeping them out. Covering ourselves with a blanket, we tried to sleep, but this was impossible, at least for me, and we all welcomed the dawn gladly, although it meant wading knee-deep in mud for nearly half a mile to get our canoe afloat. But, oh, the relief of getting away !

A Thousand Miles from a Post Office

Crossing Hannah and Rupert's Bay, at the end of six days of what was anything but a picnic, we reached East Main River, another trading post of the Hudson's Bay Company. As usual we met with a hearty welcome from the man in charge, a quaint old Scotsman, living in very primitive state. On one occasion, being asked why he kept all the windows of his house tightly closed in summer, he replied, "Aye, mon, but if ye lived here i' winter, ye wadna want any windows open at a'."

After another eight days' travel, with constant gales, thunderstorms, rain and sleet, we reached Fort George, or Big River, another trading post. It was a treat to get into a decent house again, where one could wash, sit down to a table for meals, and sleep in a comfortable bed. One gets accustomed to sleeping on the ground in all sorts of places, but a bed is always a welcome thing to anyone but an Indian.

Fort George is often spoken of as the Paradise of James Bay, and it is indeed such, compared to many other places on the Bay. Vegetables can be raised, and wild berries of all kinds grow well. The gentleman in charge let us have another canoe, which was at least watertight, and after two days' rest we started again on our journey. We met with very stormy weather, and it was now getting bitterly cold. It took us nearly a fortnight to reach the next trading post, Great Whale River, and just as we were getting into the mouth of the river we came very near ending our trip at the bottom, being caught in a gale which carried away our mast and sail, and but for the skill of our steersman we would have been upset with no chance whatever of getting ashore, for the water was icy cold. However, we came safely through and spent two pleasant days at the post.

I cannot speak too highly of the great kindness and generous hospitality of all the Hudson's Bay officers. They were always willing to do everything in their power to help us. After two days' rest, we started again on the last lap of our long journey—about sixty miles.

The first day we made good progress, running along a " sound " protected from the open sea, but after passing this we were again exposed to a severe gale, and at last were driven ashore, but fortunately managed to scramble out and save all our goods.

Being only 15 miles from Little Whale River, Mr. Peck proposed that next day we should walk in, leaving the men to bring on the canoe when the gale went down. I had always been considered a good walker, and thought that 15 miles would be nothing, but that journey is present to my mind even now.

To walk on a good hard road is not much preparation for the kind of walking we had to face. There was not even a trail, but we had to make our way through bush, over rocks, and wade through creeks up to the middle in icy cold water. We were ten hours in making that 15 miles, and once in crossing a large creek I simply dropped in up to the neck, but managed to scramble out on the other side.

The cold and this wetting gave me cramp so badly that I could hardly get on at all, but all things come to those who wait, or walk as in our case, and at last, footsore and weary, we arrived, and thus ended my first long journey in Hudson's Bay. At the time it seemed to me hard training, but in after years I looked back upon it as one of the least trying of my northern trips.

CHAPTER II

MY FIRST WINTER AMONGST THE ESKIMOS
(1882–1883)

LITTLE WHALE RIVER on the east side of Hudson's Bay is one of the dreariest places that can possibly be imagined, especially in winter. The trading post stands on a plateau of sand about a mile from the open sea; behind it rises a ridge of rocks about one hundred and fifty feet high; before it lies the river, about half a mile wide, with a very swift current.

There is no timber in the neighbourhood, only a few stunted pine-trees. The absence of vegetation is due to the extreme severity of the winter. Owing to its close proximity to the Bay, the place is exposed to the full sweep of the gales, which in winter are almost continuous.

At the time of my visit, in 1882, the post consisted of the " master's " house—a large building of two stories—a trading shop, men's house, and one or two sod shacks belonging to the Eskimos. There was also a small iron church, imported from England by Mr. Peck, in which we met regularly for service in Eskimo and English. Though life in such a place during the winter is generally very dreary and trying, I did not find it so, owing doubtless to the novelty of the surroundings, and also to the fact that I spent a very large part of my time with the Eskimos, who are wonderfully bright and cheery companions, my aim being to study the people and their language.

We took up our abode with Mr. Gillies the trader, and, being three bachelors, without cook or servant, we arranged to take a week each in providing meals. We also did our own housework, with the exception of washing the floors. Mr. Peck was a most excellent cook, and I have never met anyone who was a better breadmaker, though it was often a difficult matter to keep it warm when making, but he never followed the plan I have known adopted by settlers of the west of taking the dough to bed with him.

There were some two hundred Eskimos connected with the post at the time, but these have since been greatly reduced. Most of them had left for their hunting before we arrived, and there was only one, Old Melucto, and his family left. Old Melucto was a man of exceptionally fine character. Though very aged and infirm, he had learned to read Eskimo in syllabic characters, and nearly every day one might see him poring over his books, his face beaming as he read the good news of the Gospel.

If ever a man really and truly loved the Lord Jesus, that man was Old Melucto. Every night we had prayers in his sod shack by the light of a small blubber lamp, and it was a joy to see how the old man entered into these services.

My First Winter amongst the Eskimos

We were dependent to a very large extent upon our guns for animal food, and almost every day Peck and I, after several hours' hard grind at Eskimo, would start out after ptarmigan, which fortunately for us were very plentiful that year. It was seldom we returned without sufficient for next day's dinner. Once during these hunts I had a very narrow escape: Peck's gun caught in some branches, and the whole charge of shot passed within a few inches of my head; however, a miss is as good as a mile, and I escaped to tell the tale.

At short intervals we had to hitch up our Eskimo dogs—our only animals—and go off for firewood, for when the winter really set in, it required a large amount of wood to keep the fires alight night and day. The winds and gales came in from the Bay in icy blasts, and there were many days when it was impossible to venture out at all, even when clad in Eskimo deerskin clothing.

At Christmas-time quite a number of the Eskimos came in, and we resolved to make it a real time of rejoicing for them. With this end in view we gave them a feast. Not having much animal food at the time we decided to make a " Cossack pudding." This is simply a pudding made with large lumps of fat pork instead of suet. We boiled it in a ten-gallon kettle, and it required our united strength to get it out, for it was solid, but the Eskimos enjoyed it immensely, especially the large pieces of fat, which they regarded as titbits.

A Thousand Miles from a Post Office

When Mr. Peck came to Whale River, he endeavoured to institute a reform along the lines of a well-known proverb. He conceived the heroic project of inducing the Eskimos to wash, a thing they had never thought of doing in their lives. With this end in view, he gathered some of the men in his own little room, initiated them into the mysteries of the art, and then left them alone for a while. On his return he was unable to discover a single " shining face " among them, yet, strange to say, scarcely a vestige of the large piece of soap remained. By dint of cross-examination he found out that this had been divided amongst them and eaten !

After our feast, as it was a fine day, we all turned out to play football. The Eskimos are very fond of all kinds of games, and make good athletes. Women with babies on their backs also joined freely in the game. I was at first very much afraid to see them constantly rolled over in the snow, but they went at it again as if nothing had happened. They are all good runners, and with the greatest glee and good humour rolled one another over in the snow, reminding me of polar bears at play.

After Christmas Mr. Peck was most anxious that I should visit the Eskimos in their winter quarters, though I cannot say that I was quite as eager. However, as a party of them was staying out on a reef some fifteen or twenty miles out to sea, I decided to go and spend some days with them at their snow village.

My First Winter amongst the Eskimos

In the middle of February, on a very cold but clear day, with the thermometer nearly forty below zero, we started in the early morning with a team of six splendid husky dogs.

Some practice is required in order to master the art of driving Eskimo dogs, which are unlike Indian dogs, for every dog is hitched on a separate line, varying in length from ten to thirty feet. The dogs are born fighters, and constantly become mixed up in free fights. On these occasions it requires a very free use of the Eskimo whip in order to part them, and if the driver is not expert the long heavy whip-lash will most likely come round his own head instead of round one of the dogs. They also frequently become tangled up—that is, their traces become crossed—and a halt of ten minutes out on the frozen sea is necessary in order to extricate them and start again.

The ice at the mouth of the river was piled up in large masses, and caused us a great deal of trouble in getting over, but once out on the smooth ice of the sea, we made very good progress, and reached the snow village soon after midday. It consisted of six snow-houses with two or three families in most of them. I found one house with but one family, and with them took up my abode.

One's first attempt in living in a snow-house is an experience attended with no small degree of discomfort and repulsion. The house is round, made of large blocks of snow cut out of a snow-bank. Inside it is about twelve feet in diameter. About half of it is raised some two feet, forming a sort of dais; this is used as a living and sleeping place, being covered over with plaited willows or long dry grass. On this are laid the deerskin robes or sleeping-bags which form your bed.

The Eskimos when retiring for the night creep into these robes, slip off their garments, putting them outside to freeze, so that in the morning you can shake them and they are quite dry. The temperature is, of course, always below freezing-point; there is no fire, but a small, smelly, blubber lamp gives a dim religious light. The ventilation is nil or only such as you get from the small doorway, and at times the atmosphere becomes almost unbearable. I shall never forget the first night. I could hardly breathe. Being nearly suffocated, I at last arose and crept outside, but as it was blowing a regular blizzard, and the thermometer was nearly fifty below zero, I speedily came to the conclusion that it was better to suffocate than to freeze to death, so crept back into the *iglo*, and used the body of my Eskimo companion as a foot-warmer.

The absence of fire in their houses deprives the Eskimos of external heat, consequently they depend almost entirely upon the amount of fat or blubber they consume. As a result of this their bodies, if they are in good condition and have plenty of food, are often as hot as a glowing fire, so that there is no difficulty in keeping warm if only you have an Eskimo

ESKIMO SEAL HUNTING

ESKIMO SNOW IGLO

as a companion. I lived amongst them ten days, teaching the children during the day and holding services in the evening, when the men returned home. One day, during my stay, we had a fearful blizzard; as we were right out on the frozen sea, there was, of course, no shelter, and for the greater part of the day we could not see a dozen yards away from the *igloes*.

Upon our return we met with one or two rather exciting experiences. We were running along the smooth ice at a good pace when we came quite suddenly upon a large crack some six feet wide; the dogs just managed to pull up on to the edge of it, and we prevented the sledge going into the sea by simply turning it over on its side. Had we gone into the water we must, without doubt, have been either drowned or frozen to death, for even if we had managed to get out there was no chance of making a fire for some hours, and with the thermometer at forty below zero we must have frozen to death.

When we reached the mouth of the river we found the ice rougher than ever, and were compelled to climb over ridges fully twenty feet high. Once, when we had got to the top of one of these hummocks of ice, the dogs bolted. An Eskimo woman and her baby were sitting on the sledge at the time, and dogs, sledge, woman and baby landed in a heap at the bottom. I felt sure one or both would be killed, but they escaped without a scratch. Within half an hour of this we were safely back at the post.

A Thousand Miles from a Post Office

My stay at Little Whale River now began to draw to a close. On the whole, I had spent a very happy time there, and had succeeded in getting some knowledge of the language and a very good idea of the people. About the middle of April, when the days were getting longer, though the winter was by no means over, I started on my return journey to Moose Factory, where I had promised to be early in June. Mr. Peck and two Eskimos, with a team of dogs, were to accompany me as far as Fort George. During the day the sun was very hot, but in the late afternoons and evenings the wind was bitterly cold, and as a result our faces were blistered and very sore.

The first night was spent in an Eskimo tent, their snow-houses having now become useless. The second night we reached Great Whale River, and as it was Sunday next day, we stayed over to have service with the people, the first since the previous October. On Monday morning we resumed our journey, but a heavy fall of snow having taken place made travelling very bad, and continuous hard labour was needed to get dogs and sledge through at all.

We crossed Cape Jones, which divides Hudson's Bay from James's Bay, one of the bleakest and most dreary spots along the coast. That night we were compelled to camp under one small solitary tree, and had great difficulty in finding sufficient firewood to boil our tea-kettle; in truth it was a miserable night. Sunday we spent in a snow-storm on a bleak and barren island. It would have been much more pleasant to travel than to halt as we did, but we always refused to travel on Sundays unless it was absolutely necessary.

After eight days' very heavy travelling we reached Fort George, and I was very glad to find myself at the end of the first stage of my return journey.

Although it was now the middle of May, the ice in the river and along the coast was still as firm as a rock, and, being most desirous of pushing on, I bade farewell to Mr. Peck (whom I did not see again for over twenty years, although working in the same diocese all the time), and set out on the ice for East Main post. I arrived there without any striking incident, and again accepted the hospitality of my old friend of the closed windows. The ice was now becoming thin and dangerous, and I was forced to abandon travelling by dogs and sledge, having come some three hundred and fifty miles on my way.

A whole month was spent in the pleasant society of my Scottish friend before the opening up of the coast enabled me to start for Moose Factory. During my stay at East Main Mr. C—— invited me to go on a bear hunt with his two sons. Accordingly we started one fine day in June. In order to do honour to the missionary the old gentleman had placed a small box in the bottom of the canoe, covering it over with a flag. Unfortunately I neglected to examine this seat, which seemed to go right across the canoe. We had not gone more than a quarter of a mile when I somehow slipped off the box, and the three of us were thrown out into the greatly swollen and rapid river, and though by clinging to the canoe we managed to get ashore, all our provisions were lost. Thus our bear hunt came to an untimely end. A few days later we made another attempt, but returned without even the sight of a bear.

As soon as the ice cleared off the coast, Mr. C—— procured a canoe and two Indians for me, and we began the final stage of my long journey.

Whilst crossing Rupert's Bay, a stretch of 12 miles, we were caught in a heavy gale, and for a time were in considerable danger, but finally reached the shore with our canoe half-full of water and everything soaked. We were obliged to camp for several days until the gale was over. By pressing on as hard as we could we managed to reach Moose by the end of June, instead of at the beginning, as I had promised.

The journey from Little Whale River to Moose Fort, a distance of 500 miles, had taken more than two months.

CHAPTER III

A THREE-THOUSAND-MILE TRIP, CHIEFLY BY CANOE
(1883)

UPON my arrival at Moose I was sorry to find that Bishop Horden had been prevented from visiting Rupert's House by my late arrival, but this could not be avoided, as the coast was so late in breaking up that year. The Rev. H. Nevitt had to take the Bishop's place, and we had passed each other somewhere in Hannah Bay, but had not seen him. I was sorry to miss him.

After spending a fortnight at Moose, during which time I was ordained both deacon and priest, I prepared for another long journey to York Factory, on the western side of the Bay. The distance between the two places is only about eight hundred miles in a direct line, but there was no means of travelling up the western shore of the Bay except by canoe, and this is much too dangerous, since the land is all low-lying and swampy along those shores, with no islands to give one shelter from the sea. I was therefore obliged to make my way into the interior, travel through a large part of Canada, and then come down to the coast again; this meant a journey of nearly three thousand miles, and it took me two and a half months to reach my destination, though in a steamer, or even with a sailing vessel, the distance could have been covered in three or four days.

A small birchbark canoe, manned by three men, conveyed me up the Missinābie branch of the Moose River. A large number of portages were necessary at places where the rapids and falls were too formidable for tracking or poling, but we got through without any great difficulty or mishap. On our fourteenth day from Moose we reached Brunswick House, a few miles from the present station of Missinābie on the Canadian Pacific Railway. Here I had my first and only trouble with Indians. My three men had been supplied with twenty-one days' rations when we left Moose, and now, at the end of fourteen days, they had no "grub" left, though we had still five or six days to travel in order to reach Michepecoton on Lake Superior. Fortunately I had a fairly good supply of my own, not having used mine so freely as the men had theirs, and so we were able to get through without more inconvenience than having to go on rather short rations. In running a rather dangerous rapid just before reaching Michepecoton we had a most exciting time: our canoe was half-filled with water and all my books, clothing, etc., were soaked. This prevented us reaching the post that night, and we had to spend a very uncomfortable time on a long portage, and then go into the Hudson's Bay post next morning, which was Sunday. As usual we met with the warmest welcome from the officer in charge, and spent a very pleasant day there waiting for the steamer to take us into Port Arthur, the western extremity of Lake Superior. Michepecoton was at that time just a trading post of the Hudson's Bay Company, visited by a steamer once a week or so. It has since become quite a large mining centre, and now presents a very different appearance.

The day after our arrival the steamer coming in, we went on board, and next day reached Port Arthur, or Prince Arthur's Landing as it was then called. The town of Fort William was as yet non-existent, and the Canadian Pacific Railway had been completed only between Port Arthur and Winnipeg.

This was the first western town I had ever seen, and it struck me as very strange indeed. The railway ran right up the centre of the main street, and the town itself consisted of a few shacks thrown down, or rather up, just anyhow. The few hours I stayed here before taking the night train for Winnipeg were not spent in sight-seeing, since everything could very easily be seen in five minutes. As we travelled by night I had no chance of seeing anything of the country until in the early morning we ran into Rat Portage, now Kenora, on the Lake of the Woods, one of the prettiest lakes in Central Canada. Here there seemed to be little besides the railway station, a very poor affair, and one or two other buildings, chief amongst which, as usual in a western town, was the hotel or saloon. Altogether the place was very different from the pretty little town of Kenora as it is to-day, where I have had the honour and privilege of living for the last eighteen years.

Winnipeg had just passed through the boom of 1882, and was still feeling the ill-effects. The town in those days consisted of one main street, with very narrow sidewalks. The mud in the roadway was ankle-deep, and of a singularly adhesive character. If one had to cross the street, it was necessary on the farther side to examine one's foot-gear carefully to make sure one had not left it behind on the way across. At the present day it is almost impossible to realize what the place was like forty years ago.

I spent three days as the guest of the late Primate, Archbishop Machray (then only Bishop of Rupert's Land), at old Bishop's Court, with its many memories of Bishop Anderson, its first Bishop, and the early missionaries of Red River country.

Old St. John's School was then standing, but now all the old buildings have gone, the ancient land-marks have been removed, and even Bishop's Court has given place to a new and modern building.

A single small steamer then ran on Lake Winnipeg, one of the small lakes of Canada, only 300 miles long, at rather irregular intervals. For this I had to wait nearly a month, and during that time was most hospitably entertained by the Rev.

A Three-Thousand-Mile Trip

R. Young and his good wife at St. Andrew's. The following year the Rev. R. Young was consecrated the second Bishop of Athabasca. This gave me an excellent opportunity of becoming acquainted with some of the old Red River settlers, such as the late Captain Kennedy, with whom I passed many pleasant evenings (listening to tales of his northern trips), John Norquay, first Premier of Manitoba, Archdeacon Cowley, and many others.

I was most impatient to get on, but things did not move at all quickly in those days, and there was nothing to do but wait for the steamer. At the end of nearly a month a " runner " came up from Selkirk to say that the boat was in, and would start out early in the morning, so I had to take a very hasty leave of my host and hostess, whose kindness I have never forgotten, and take a " rig " to catch the *Princess*.

There was quite a large party on board and not too much room; amongst the passengers were the Ven. Archdeacon Cowley, going to visit the Missions at Cumberland House and other places; Mr. and Mrs. Cuthbert Sinclair of Oxford House, with whom I was to travel as far as that place; and a party of about a dozen tourists going to see the lake. The accommodation was poor and scanty, and the very rough weather we encountered was not at all conducive to comfort. I remember well that one morning the captain and I were the only ones to face the ordeal of the breakfast table. A voyage of

25

nearly a week brought us at last to Warren's Landing at the outlet of the Nelson River from the lake. The Sinclairs, a Methodist minister and his family, and I disembarked here, with 20 miles still before us ere we should reach Norway House. An Indian at work cutting hay, to whom we applied for means of water transport, informed us that he had only a small canoe. We were therefore obliged to dispatch him to Norway House in search of a large boat. It was not until the end of the third day that his successful return enabled us to continue our journey.

Norway House was in those days, and is still, an important post of the Hudson's Bay Company, but gone for ever is the glory of the early days when the " Councils of the North " were held there, with Sir George Simpson in the chair, surrounded by his chief factors and traders—the three grades of officers in the Company's service.

The fort stands in a very conspicuous position on a rocky point overlooking the Jack River where it empties into Little Playgreen Lake. It is surrounded by a rather low stockade of wood, with a very imposing gateway. All the buildings are of wood, whitewashed or painted. Inside there stand two rows of warehouses, etc.; the " Master's House " is at the upper end overlooking the whole, and " Bachelors' Hall " close by.

Four miles across the lake is the Methodist Mission attached to the Indian village there, one

INDIAN SHAK

NORWAY HOUSE TRADING POST

of the oldest Indian Missions in the whole north country. Here Mr. Evans, an early missionary, invented that wonderful syllabic system in which so many Indian books are printed and which has been such a boon to the whole north country. Here also Dr. Mason, for many years a C.M.S. Missionary at York Factory, began his work amongst the Cree Indians. Ordained afterwards as a minister of the Church of England, he, with the assistance of his wife, translated the whole Bible into the Cree language. This work formed the basis of Archdeacon Mackay's revision, which was completed in 1908.

Leaving Norway House after a stay of a week— during which I had the privilege of preaching to a large number of Christian Indians in the Methodist church—we made our way to Oxford House in a York boat, a very much more comfortable method of travel than by canoe. For some thirty miles we went down the Nelson River, then up the Ichemarmis, a very small and narrow river flowing into the Nelson, then across a small height of land, into lakes and rivers flowing in a more easterly direction leading into the Hill River, and finally into the Hayes.

Oxford House is another Methodist mission station. There being no minister in charge at the time of my visit, I was asked to give them a service, which I was much pleased to do, and I also baptized several children

A Thousand Miles from a Post Office

The journey from Oxford House to York Factory was made in a small birchbark canoe with two Indians. During this part of the trip we encountered a very large number of rapids, some of them very difficult to run and some quite impossible. Running rapids in the north country is most exciting and dangerous work. At first one sits in fear and trembling, but after a time the fear passes and one takes it as a mere matter of course, yet the danger is a very real one, though overcome to a wonderful extent by the great skill of the natives in handling their canoes. Of course accidents and some deaths by drowning occur now and then, but they are very few and far between with native boatmen, and much more frequent in the case of white men, who imagine they can handle a canoe as well as a native. In the very first rapid we had the misfortune to run our canoe on to a rock, thereby tearing a hole in the birchbark about a foot long. We just managed to get ashore with our canoe more than half-full of water and all our baggage soaking wet. One learns to take this sort of thing very philosophically after a time in northern travel.

The damage was rapidly and skilfully repaired. One Indian built a big fire whilst the other went off into the woods and returned with a large piece of birchbark torn off a tree. This was sewn over the rent with willow roots, and the edges covered over with pitch, which we carried for the purpose. In an hour we were afloat again, as if nothing had

28

happened. No other exciting incident happened to us, except that we fell in with a large herd of deer; however, having no bullets, we were unable to shoot any of them, though we were very short of food at the time.

The weather became very bad as we neared the coast; snow fell every day, and the water froze on our paddles as we strained every nerve to reach the Bay before the winter really set in.

On the 2nd of October we came in sight of York Factory. It presented a very wintry appearance, the ground being thickly covered with snow, and sharp frosts occurring every night. More than five months had elapsed since I left Little Whale River, which, in actual distance across the Bay, was little more than five hundred miles from York. Though still 200 miles from Churchill, my future home, I was glad to be thus far on my journey and on the west side of the Bay. I had spent fourteen weeks in actual travel, either by snow-shoe or in canoe; during this time I never slept in a bed, and had covered over three thousand miles.

The Rev. G. S. Winter was in charge of the Mission at York, and he and his good wife gave me a very hearty welcome. It was a great change to them to have the prospect of a fellow-worker for the winter, for the next missionary was some six hundred miles away. To my very great disappointment I found that there was no possibility of my going on to Churchill that year. The annual ship had been and left again for the north, and, until the freezing up of the lakes and rivers made travelling by snow-shoes and sledge possible, all communication with the more northern post was cut off, so after all my exertions and toil I had failed in reaching my goal. One of the great things that one learns in the north is not to " count your chickens before they are hatched."

CHAPTER IV

A WINTER AT YORK FACTORY
(1883-1884)

YORK FORT, or Factory as it is more generally called, situated on the Hayes River about four miles from its junction with the Nelson, has, ever since the formation of the Hudson's Bay Company in 1670, been one of their most important posts, especially so before the opening of the Canadian Pacific Railway, when it was the depot of the whole western country, and York boats came here not only from Fort Frances, Winnipeg, and the surrounding country, but from Edmonton and the far-away Mackenzie River.

The first settlers of Red River, sent out by Lord Selkirk, entered the country through this port, and after spending one winter at York, and evidently suffering great hardships, left York Factory on the 6th of July for the interior, and they only arrived at Fort Garry on the 30th of August, having had a terrible time coming up the rivers from the coast and across Lake Winnipeg. The arrival of the annual ship at York was the great event of the year, and might take place any time between the middle of August and the end of September, according to the state of the ice in the Strait and Bay. At that time forty or fifty chief factors, factors, chief traders, and traders would assemble at York from all parts to obtain their yearly supplies and to send home to England the furs they had collected during the winter. Then, indeed, it was a busy scene on the banks of the Hayes.

The present fort is only one left of the three or four that were built by the Company on the swampy land forming the peninsula between the Hayes and Nelson Rivers, and either abandoned because of their unsanitary position or burnt down. It is stockaded, as was usual with all their forts, and boasts, or rather did boast in 1883, six large gateways, which were all closed and locked at dark. The large storehouse which stands in the centre is one of the finest buildings in the Hudson's Bay regions, and is capable of containing supplies for the whole of the trading posts.

At one time a staff of twenty clerks and nearly one hundred men, coopers, tinsmiths, boat-builders, and carpenters, were in regular employment, and in summer nearly all the Indians were also employed, but even in 1883 the place had begun to decline, and now its glory has departed.

In the early days, many of the missionaries and clergy brought out to this country in the Company's vessels acted as chaplains, but it was not until 1854 that actual mission work was commenced at York, when Bishop Anderson sent in the Rev. W. Mason, who had been a Methodist missionary at Norway House. The translation of the Bible into Cree was to a very large extent the work of Mrs. Mason, who was a native of Red River, had grown up amongst the Indians, and understood their language perfectly. It is the most idiomatic and by far the best translation that has ever been made in Cree. At York Factory Mrs. Mason on her dying bed finished the last chapter of this marvellous book, which has been such a blessing to the Indians of the whole north country.

Both Dr. Mason and the Ven. Archdeacon Kirkby, who succeeded him, did splendid and lasting work, and their names are well remembered to this day.

Connected with the post at the time of my arrival there were some five or six hundred Indians living the story-book life of hunting and fishing. For this purpose they travelled very great distances, some of them only coming to the fort once a year for trading purposes. During the short summer most of the Indians were kept employed about the place, not so much for the value of the work they did, as for the purpose of preventing them from killing the fur-bearing animals out of season, for in the north the " close season " has always been strictly observed.

When the Indians are in at the post, the missionary is kept very busy indeed. It was quite common, even in 1883, to see congregations of from two to three hundred or even more at a service. In this the Indians joined most heartily, for nearly all of them could read in their own tongue, though very few of them knew anything of English. Family prayers seemed to be a regular institution, there being scarcely a house or tent in which they were not said both night and morning; thus religion was made a part of their daily life. I found the first part of the winter slip away pleasantly and swiftly assisting the missionary in day-school—which was in the north always a part of one's duty—and in the daily services and visiting.

Christmas and New Year's Day, especially the latter, were always great events in the north. Everyone seemed bent on doing his or her best to make them a time of happiness and rejoicing. On New Year's Day the fort was alive with people very early in the morning, for every house had to be visited and tea and cake indulged in. A peculiar custom was that every man was expected to kiss every woman and girl in the place, and it was sometimes most amusing to see how this was managed.

Shortly after Christmas the great event of the winter took place in the arrival of the " packet " from Winnipeg. This was hauled all the way by Indians on flat sledges or toboggans, and generally took about six weeks. Only those who have been without news of the outer world for three or four months can understand what this means, and the crowds who gathered in the guard-room were an amusing, and in some respects a pathetic, sight.

Early in February, the " packet " from Churchill

also arrived with the rather doleful news that the annual ship, a sailing vessel, had been frozen in at that post, and the captain and crew were detained there for the winter. She had been very late in leaving York, and only reached Churchill on the 10th of October, by which time the ground was covered with a foot of snow, and it seemed as if the winter had really set in, so that the captain did not think it wise to put out again for fear of being frozen in before he got through the Hudson's Strait.

This event, unfortunate as it was in many respects, gave me an opportunity of going on to Churchill for a short visit. It was true that the journey would consist of a run on snow-shoes of 400 miles, 200 each way, but by this time I thought very little of such an expedition, and was overjoyed at the chance of going.

In the middle of February, accompanied by Dr. P. Matthews of the Hudson's Bay Company, we started out from York. The weather was bitterly cold, the glass showing forty degrees below zero and a strong north-west wind blowing in our faces the whole way. The usual route (there is no trail) is to cross the Nelson, at a point where it is about seven miles wide, and then to skirt the shores of the bay almost up to Cape Churchill. Along the whole route there is very little shelter of any kind, and often at night-time we were obliged to go four or five miles out of our way before we could find a camping-place and firewood.

A Thousand Miles from a Post Office

Tents are never carried in the north country in the winter, and you sleep out in the open in a hole dug in the snow and covered over with the branches of trees, with a large fire—when you can get one—in the front. In this cold and cheerless method of camping (which is really comfortable enough in a well-wooded country), you crawl into your deer or rabbit skin robes and try to sleep until four or five in the morning, by which time you are only too glad to turn out and put on a fire, if you can find wood to burn. Oftentimes in such a camp the only way of getting at all warm is to make a " spit " of one's self, and keep on turning round in front of the fire, for as fast as one part warms up the other part freezes.

We had very bad weather the whole way, and the noses and cheeks of our whole party were very badly frozen when we at last reached Churchill on our sixth day. We must, indeed, have been a rough-looking lot on our arrival, but our sore feet and frozen limbs were soon forgotten in the warm welcome we received from Mr. and Mrs. John Spencer, who were in charge. Mr. Spencer was a brother of Mr. M. Spencer, whom I had met the year before at Fort George, and his wife was a sister of Archdeacon Phair of Winnipeg, so we had many friends in common.

Churchill in winter is a very dreary place and far from attractive. It consisted at that time of the " master's house," a comfortable dwelling of good size, a small one-roomed habitation for the clerk, in which he both worked and slept, three very dilapidated houses for the men, and but three other buildings in the place—viz., the store, shop, and blubber-house.   I stayed here just a month, holding services and teaching school in the master's house, there being no other place I could use.   There were about a dozen English sailors from the *Ocean Nymph* at the post, and a mixed multitude (about fifty) of English, Irish, Scotch, half-breeds, Indians, and Eskimos, so that I found plenty of work to do. Many of the sailors were down with scurvy, some of them very bad.   This was brought on almost entirely by the lazy life they led.   They were so terribly afraid of the cold that they hardly put their noses out of doors, and would not take sufficient exercise, having no regular work to do. Up to that time I had believed, with most people, that scurvy was produced chiefly by living upon salt food, but my opinion on this point underwent a complete change, for these sailors were living on much better food than the residents of the fort; they had a good supply of fresh meat brought from the ship, with flour and vegetables, whilst the people of the fort were living almost entirely on salt meat, as game was very scarce about the place that year; they had very little flour, as the Company did not import much in those days, and eight pounds of flour was the week's allowance for a family of eight or nine persons; and they had no vegetables, as these are not grown and are never imported by the Company. Yet, in spite of all this, whilst the sailors were all down with scurvy, and had been so for weeks, there was only one case of it amongst the fort people, an old man over eighty, who was unable to get about. The reason for this was simply that the fort people led very active lives and went off in the woods to get food or cut firewood, etc., whilst the sailors, as I have said, would not move out of the house.

After spending a very happy month at Churchill I tramped back to York. The weather was now much milder, and travelling with, instead of against, the wind we got on much faster, and arrived at York on the fifth day with nothing worse than blistered feet caused by the hard walking and a touch of snow-blindness due to the intense glare of the sun on the snow.

CHAPTER V

A GREAT AND TRYING DISAPPOINTMENT

(1884)

On my return from Churchill in March I settled down again to steady work, helping the Rev. G. S. Winter in his labours at York Factory, sharing the teaching in the day-school, visi. ng the tents of the Indians, and taking my share in preaching at both the English and Indian services.

A few weeks later the spring packet arrived from the interior. The absence of all news from the outside world for a period of three months or more causes the arrival of the mail to be greeted with the greatest excitement imaginable, though it is remarkable that after a time in the north one does not think much of one's isolation until the mail actually arrives. Then one's hunger for news is assuaged, there is a great rush for the letters, and their contents form the sole topic of conversation for weeks after. Most of my letters by this mail contained good news; from one letter I learned that my affianced wife was to come out by the ship in August to throw in her lot with mine, and to join me in working for the good of the Eskimos and Indians. The long months of waiting from April

39

to August did not seem to drag along so slowly as one might have feared, for in the lonely fastnesses of the north time flies much more quickly than one would dare to hope.

Spring came on very early that year, bringing with it first of all the pretty little snow bunting in countless numbers, and the children were all very busy trying to net them for food. These harbingers of spring appear to migrate north and south, all the time keeping, as it were, upon the edge of the snow.

Then followed the geese, which fly along the shores of the Bay in spring to return in the autumn, surer weather prophets than even the great " Foster." Since the rapid development of the west, however, the geese seem to have discovered the grain fields, and follow a fresh route to the north, where they go to nest and raise their young, for they are by no means so plentiful as formerly on the shores of the Bay. In past times, at all the posts, people used to depend upon the geese for their supply of fresh food both in the spring and fall, shooting them oftentimes in thousands.

The opening of the Hayes River followed soon after the flight of the birds. This was an event always awaited with some anxiety, for the ice will sometimes jam in the river, causing it to rise and flood the whole countryside ; even the fort itself is sometimes inundated to the depth of a foot or two, and large blocks of ice come crashing right up against the stockades or pickets. Parts of the

HUDSON'S BAY TRADING POST

p. 4

river bank are often carried away and great damage is done.

The Indians follow closely in the wake of the ice, many of them floating down just behind it on rafts of timber and firewood. All is then bustle and excitement; the work of the summer has begun. English school gives place to Indian, services are held every night, and there is a constant stream of the dusky children of the woods to see and consult the missionary upon the thousand and one points which may have arisen since their last visit to the fort. Generally there is quite a large number of children to be baptized, and nearly always several marriages have to be performed.

The annual ship was to call first of all at Churchill that year, and, as I did not like the idea of a young lady landing in a strange country with no one she knew to welcome her, I decided to go on there to meet her.

The only possible means of travel at that time of the year—July—was to tramp along the shores of the Bay. There were no roads or trails, no stopping-places, not a house of any kind between York and Churchill, but I was by this time accustomed to roughing it, and thought no more of a walk of 200 miles than of one of 20 in the Old Country, more especially so on this occasion when I had the realization of a long-expected meeting in prospect.

Accompanied by two Indians, a man, and a boy, each carrying a blanket, gun, and a few pounds of hard tack, a little tea, and sugar, we started across the Nelson on the 26th of July in one of the Hudson's Bay Company's boats. A very heavy thunderstorm overtook us as we rounded the "Point of Marsh," between the Hayes and Nelson Rivers, and for a time our lives were in great danger. We got across in safety, however, and encamped in a creek on the far side of the 17-mile stretch of river. Next morning the boat returned to York, and we began our tramp north.

The western coast of Hudson's Bay is very flat and swampy, especially between York and Churchill. Owing to the lack of any road or trail the walking is often very wet and rough, so we camped that night at Stoney Creek, both stiff and tired out. Having no tent, we were obliged to sleep out in the open with no other protection than that of a rude driftwood screen to windward and a big fire in the front. Next day our guide, Andrew Flett, succeeded in killing a deer. This supply of fresh meat was most opportune, for we had very little with us; we were, however, unable to take very much, as it would have added greatly to our already heavy burdens.

I was trudging slowly along, deep in conversation with my Indian boy, when quite suddenly he stopped and whispered, "Look, a bear!" Taken unawares, and unable for the moment to see anything, I thought he was jesting until with his outstretched chin and finger he pointed out a large polar bear sound asleep in a clump of sedge grass not twenty yards away. His big white sides rose and fell with bellows-like regularity.

With a keenness readily understood I was preparing to shoot him when Andrew, whose heavier load had delayed him somewhat, came up and objected most strongly to my doing so. He pointed out, quite rightly, that we could not carry more than what we already had with us, that we required no more meat, and that we were 100 miles from anywhere. As this was the first polar bear I had seen, I was by no means willing to be convinced, but at length allowed his emphatic " No, no use kill him, not shoot, no carry skin to Churchill " to dissuade me. Accordingly we drew off a few paces to windward and Andrew told me to fire just over his back. Up he jumped, as scared as a jack-rabbit, and made for the open water with great lumbering strides, never so much as glancing round to see what had frightened him, although we were not twenty yards away. The next day we saw another polar bear, but he was a long way off and was making for the open sea.

This portion of the coast is a very good place for bears. I have gone along there dozens of times and hardly ever without seeing two or three, sometimes fishing off Cape Churchill, and sometimes on the shore.

After eight days' very heavy travelling, sometimes plunging through swamps, up to the knees in water, at other times walking on the sharp limestone with which the coast is strewn, spending the night wherever it happened to overtake us, often drenched to the skin by heavy rain and sleeping in our wet garments, we at length reached Churchill, where the warm welcome of Mr. J. Spencer and his genial Irish wife, and the luxuries of a bath and a comfortable bed, soon made me forget my aching limbs and badly blistered feet.

The late arrival of the annual ship, which did not appear until the end of August, caused much anxiety at Churchill, and to none more so than to me. Any delay in the coming of the one ship a year is naturally a matter of great concern to people who are dependent upon it for their supply of food and clothing. However, one day, at the cry of " The ship is in sight," all the inhabitants gathered on the high rocks at the back of the post, from which one has an extensive view of the Bay. With deep thankfulness we watched the ship make her way into the snug little harbour, and soon after she had cast anchor Mr. Spencer and I went on board.

As we climbed up the side of the vessel there were no passengers visible, and I began to wonder why this was so, but thought that possibly the young lady did not like to put in an appearance and was keeping in the background. I anxiously asked if there were no passengers on board, and Captain Main at once replied in the negative. I could not believe him and rushed below, but found not a trace of anyone.

44

A Great and Trying Disappointment

When I reappeared on the deck the captain gave me a letter which very much upset me; it told me that the young lady had not come, the Company having at the very last moment refused to bring her out, as the vessel lacked the proper accommodation for her She had cabled to me to this effect, but the message only reached me upon my return to York, fully three months after it had been sent off.

My walk of 200 miles had been all in vain. There was nothing for it but to return, a sadder if not a wiser man, having learned another lesson of the patience which the north so truly teaches. Yet the time consumed on this fruitless quest was not altogether wasted. The Eskimos and Indians were greatly pleased to have a missionary amongst them, if only for a month. I had also the great pleasure and profit of meeting the Canadian Government Expedition, under the command of Commander Gordon, sent out to ascertain the possibility of navigating Hudson's Strait and Bay. Dr. Robert Bell, of the Geological Survey, was also on board. Both gentlemen were exceedingly kind to me, and took the warmest interest in the work of the Mission. This interest greatly benefited the establishment of the Churchill Mission, for their promise of every possible assistance was abundantly fulfilled in the following year. We owe a great debt of gratitude to both these gentlemen for their help and encouragement at a time when things looked about as dark as they well could be.

A Thousand Miles from a Post Office

Captain Main very kindly saved me the tramp back to York by offering me a passage in his vessel. We started out, and, after a splendid run of three days, safely anchored in "5-fathom" hole in the mouth of the Hayes, and I found myself once more under the hospitable roof of the mission house.

CHAPTER VI

(1885)

THE Rev. G. S. Winter and his family, who had been six years at York, returned to England, on furlough, about the middle of September in the *Cam Owen*, leaving me in charge of the work at the Mission, but my bachelor life was vastly more pleasant than it had been at Whale River, as I had the Winters' house and the services of a fairly capable Indian girl.

The winter came on as usual, and passed both swiftly and pleasantly. With all the work of the Mission on my hands, my time was fully occupied, but, nevertheless, I was able to take part in several hunting trips, during which I visited some Indian families and held services with them.

Long trips were, of course, out of the question, as I could not leave the fort for any great length of time.

When the winter packet arrived in January, I was greatly cheered by the news that my fiancée was to come out by the annual ship in the following August. Arrangements had been made, the Company had promised to bring her, and there was very little doubt she would arrive in time.

A Thousand Miles from a Post Office

Spring came on very slowly that year, or, at least, it seemed so to me: weeks and months dragged wearily along, and it was not until the end of July that I was able to plan another walk along the coast to Churchill to meet the ship. Accompanied once more by a man and a boy, though not the same pair I had before, we left York on the 3rd of August. No boat being obtainable from the Company to put us across the Nelson River, we were obliged to wade through the 4 miles of swamp between the Hayes and the Nelson up to the knees in water, with an occasional and unexpected drop waist-deep. There is no danger of being unable to touch bottom in these swamps, for the frost never leaves them; you may go down 3 feet or so, and then come on to the solid ice—in fact, anywhere near York if you dig down 3 feet you come upon frozen ground, for the summers are not long enough or hot enough to thaw it out.

When we reached the Nelson and had gone up some miles we were fortunate enough to find several Indian families, with whom we spent the night, and next day they very kindly paddled us across the river on to the north bank. A wet and cold day's march brought us tired out and weary to Stoney River, where we spent the night in a rainstorm, which soon saturated our blankets, for we had no means of making any shelter. Day after day we trudged on. Nearly every day rain fell heavily, and it was anything but comfortable.

Patience Rewarded at Last

Game was very scarce; we met with no deer, and only once did we see a polar bear, and he was far out of reach.

On these trips we depended almost entirely upon our guns for food, as it was impossible to carry baggage weighing more than a few pounds, and there are no houses at which one can purchase supplies. I often thought with envy of the string of porters by which the missionary in Central Africa is generally accompanied, and the villages on the way where one can buy food. At the end of our fifth day, when we were still 50 miles away from Churchill, our food supply came to an end, and no game of any kind appeared. All the next day we tramped on the strength of a cup of tea. To make matters worse, the walking was simply wretched, and rain fell heavily, so that an hour after we started we were soaked to the skin; yet there was no possibility of stopping, for we had neither food nor shelter, and there was no chance of getting any until we reached Churchill unless we fell in with game. The following day was Sunday, but it was impossible to stop, so after a light breakfast of tea we started out, and trudged on until late in the afternoon, when I saw three ducks in a small pond; of these I managed to bag two. This was the only occasion on which I ever did any shooting on Sunday, but our condition was such that my conscience found nothing blameworthy in the action. We camped for the night, and had our first meal for two whole days. We did not reach Churchill until the ninth day, completely tired out, footsore and weary, and faint with hunger. The ship had not yet arrived, so that my patience was tried yet a little further.

On Sunday, the last day of August, the ship hove in sight, and as soon as she was anchored I jumped on board, and rejoiced to find there was to be no disappointment this time, for the young lady was leaning over the bulwarks to welcome me. I then learned that they had been just twelve weeks out from London, six of which had been spent fast in the ice of Hudson's Strait. As the *Cam Owen*— a small whaling vessel—boasted very little in the way of comfort or convenience, my fiancée and her maid, the only passengers, were delighted to find themselves, as they thought, at the end of their journey. The 200 miles to York Factory, however, still remained to be traversed.

We at once landed and went up to Mrs. Spencer's. The trip had been a very trying one in every way, and my fiancée had suffered greatly. When we were walking up the fort one of Mrs. Spencer's little girls rushed into the house to her mother, and said, " Oh, mother, what a narrow wife," meaning how very thin and poorly my future wife looked. In talking over affairs that night, a peculiar dilemma arose. Very briefly it was this. Mr. Winter, who we had also expected was coming out by the ship, had not arrived; his wife had been ill and his furlough had been extended. Who was to marry us ? I was the only minister in the whole of that north country. The young lady was very naturally greatly troubled at this state of affairs after a journey of 3,000 miles in a small whaler. She asked me if there was not, at least, a Methodist minister within reach who could tie the knot. I told her there certainly was, but unfortunately he was quite 700 miles away, a six weeks' journey without any possibility of returning for, at least, a year. To this she replied, if that was the case, the only possible course was for her to return to England as she had come. This plan I most emphatically vetoed. " Here you are," I said, " and here you will remain; if there is no other way out I shall perform the ceremony myself." This I knew had been done before in the north, and I was quite willing to test the legality of the question if there was no other way out of the difficulty.

At this juncture an event occurred which enabled us to find a way out. On the 2nd of September the *Alert*, the famous Arctic exploring vessel, came into the Churchill harbour, having been chartered by the Canadian Government for the second expedition to Hudson's Bay. My good friend Commander Gordon was in charge of her, together with Dr. Robert Bell and quite a large party of surveyors, amongst others Mr. J. W. Tyrrell of the Geological Survey, who was to spend the coming winter watching the ice in Hudson's Strait.

I immediately made known our difficulty to

Captain Gordon and Dr. Bell, and we finally decided that the captain should perform the ceremony on board the *Alert*, for he possessed the necessary legal qualifications, both as the captain of a naval vessel and as a magistrate for the district of Keewatin; so on Friday, September the 4th, we were married, according to the Rites of the Church of England, in the main saloon of the *Alert*, the ceremony being recorded in the ship's log and in the marriage register which she carried.

Commander Gordon and Dr. Bell, both of them most warmly interested in the work of the Churchill Mission, had brought out in the *Alert* from Ottawa a sufficient amount of lumber, with doors, windows, and stove, to make a nice little mission house. These supplies were contributed for the most part by Ottawa people, many or most of whom were Presbyterians: the first time, I imagine, that a Church of England Mission was really established by Presbyterians, for if this lumber, etc., had not been brought out, we could not have had a Mission there for years, as the Company would not help us.

As the missionary for York Factory had not arrived by the ship, we were ordered to return there and carry on the work for another year. The lumber which had been brought out for the mission house had to be landed as best it could. Commander Gordon kindly lent me some of his men, and we made a raft of about half of it, and this was towed up to Cockles Point; the other half was landed at

" The Shanty " and thrown upon the beach, where
it had to remain for a year.

A few hours after our marriage we said good-bye
to all our kind friends at the post and on board the
Alert, and put out to sea in the *Cam Owen* with the
expectation of reaching York in three or four days
at least, but nothing is more uncertain than travelling
in Hudson's Bay in September in a sailing vessel.
Scarcely had we left the harbour when we encountered a most severe gale, which compelled us to beat
up and down the coast for fourteen days. Twice
we sighted the beacon at the mouth of the Hayes
and Nelson Rivers, but we dared not go near on
account of the dangerous sand-bars in the narrow
channel.

The accommodation on board the *Cam Owen* was
very primitive and very limited, and any degree of
comfort was quite out of the question. Mrs. L.,
who is a very poor sailor at any time, was very ill
all the way, the result doubtless of her long sea
voyage in the whaler, so that when at last we did
get into the York roadstead and the Company's
boat came off to us, we were deeply thankful to
get ashore and take up our abode in the mission
house. Thus it was that my wife found her first
home not, as she expected, at Churchill, but at
York Factory.

It seemed very hard at the time to have to delay
the establishing of the Churchill Mission, but it was
really a good thing in the end, for I am quite sure

my wife's health would not have stood the strain at Churchill that winter. At York we had a doctor, and things were very comfortable compared with what they would have been at the more northern post. Thus we saw how God, even when we think things are hard, overrules all for good.

CHAPTER VII

THE FOUNDING OF THE CHURCHILL MISSION
(1885–1886)

A VERY congenial little community of English-speaking people at York made the winter of 1885–86 pass quite pleasantly. There was a resident doctor and his wife, who was a daughter of Archdeacon Kirkby, Dr. Mason's successor, also Mr. M. Matherson, of the H.B.C., and his wife, and several very nice families and clerks. The weather was remarkably mild right up to Christmas, but in the north sooner or later winter arrives with inexorable certainty.

We had also some visitors from Winnipeg very late in the year. It is interesting to note, in view of the present-day agitation for the Hudson's Bay line, that these were surveyors for the railway, but their survey consisted of a few days' stay at York and a prompt return to Oxford House.

Our winter and spring packets came and went as usual, bringing no very startling news from the outer world, but in July a packet from the interior brought the welcome news that Archdeacon Winter and his family were to return from England by the ship, and that we were at liberty to set our faces to the north. I had now been three years in the country without an opportunity of starting the Mission for which I had come to Hudson's Bay.

There had been an unfortunate dispute with the Company's officer in charge at York in regard to the establishment of a Mission at Churchill, and on this account Mr. Matherson declined to give us a passage in the Company's boat, which was going on there, or to assist us in any way.

Finally, however, he consented to our hiring a boat and crew, and, on the 21st of July, we left York and set out for Churchill, " the last house in the world."

Our boat contained six Indians, my wife, myself, and an English maid. There was no cabin or shelter of any kind, except such as we could make from sail or oil cloth. Some faint impression of the discomforts of a voyage along the shores of Hudson's Bay between York and Churchill may be gathered from the words of a recent traveller, who says, " The trip along the coast is invariably fraught with considerable exposure, and always with danger. At many points along the barren shores the tide recedes from one to four miles from the high-water mark, and it is very difficult to reach the shore for camping at night. Added to this is the difficulty of finding shelter (and fresh water), there being few places along the coast to afford spots of refuge in times of storm " (which are very frequent).

At night we ran our boat close inshore until she grounded, a rather primitive method of camping, but as the boat generally grounded a mile or two from the beach, with mud-flats in between, which a lady could not possibly traverse, there was nothing for it but to spend the nights on board.

Fortunately for us the weather remained mostly fair, and after a six days' run we reached Churchill, where we met with the usual warm welcome from the inhabitants. Having no house or even tent of our own we gratefully accepted the hospitality of the Spencers until we could render habitable a small iron church, which had been sent on from York some years before by Archdeacon Kirkby. This church, about twenty by sixteen feet, was in a sorry state of dilapidation, and did not look very promising for an abode. It was, however, the only possible home until I could put up the recently imported mission house. A curtain, hung across the centre, divided it into two rooms, one a combination living-room and bedroom, the other a kitchen. It was really a fortunate thing that in those days we possessed very few worldly goods, for the little we had occupied most of the floor space.

As this was the only place in which services could be held, everything possible was packed away on Sundays, chiefly on the bed, and seats were brought in from outside. In this manner our three Sunday services were regularly held. In the three months during which we lived in this tiny church a great deal of rain fell, and it rained almost as much inside as out, because the roof was so bad. Every utensil which could be pressed into service was in constant use to catch the dripping water. During service it was by no means an uncommon thing to see some member of the congregation, exasperated by the tantalizing drip, drip of the water on one portion of his or her body, shift to some other spot, to enjoy the relief of having a fresh part slowly saturated. In early October the thermometer went down to zero, and even below every night, and bread, butter, and everything liquid became frozen solid. I have known a kettle full of water boiling at 11 p.m. become solid ice at 5 a.m. Bed and blankets alone kept out the cold.

Our greatest concern at this time was naturally the erection of the mission house. The *Alert*, with Commander Gordon and Dr. Bell on board, had come into the harbour soon after our arrival at Churchill. Admiral Markham was also on board, having taken the voyage simply for the sake of being on board his old vessel, sailing in northern waters.

The lumber for the mission house, brought out the previous year, as already related, had been lying throughout the winter on the banks of the river, some of it at Cockles Point, 2 miles away from where the Mission was to stand, and some 5 miles away at the Whaling Shanty. We had no boat or any other means of getting it up the river, as we were not allowed to use the boat and men brought on from York, neither could we hire a man or boat from the

The Founding of the Churchill Mission

Company. However, my feeling of despair was alleviated when Captain Gordon lent me two men, with whose aid a raft was constructed of the lumber lying at the Shanty. This was towed up to the Mission by the ship's steam launch, and then, the *Alert* having to depart for York, I was left to do the best I could. With the aid of my wife I carried all the lumber brought up from the Shanty from the beach, to where I wished to build the house, a distance of 100 yards, but was unable to begin the building itself, as part of the lumber was still 2 miles away at Cockles Point. How to get this up I did not know, but early in August a party of eight Eskimos came in from the north, and I got them to go down with me and make a raft. The Churchill being a tidal river, I thought we might possibly float this up to the Mission, but I failed to take into account the fact that the Eskimos, living as they do on the treeless barren lands, know nothing of rafting lumber, and I had no experience of this work either. However, one somehow learns many things in the north, and we constructed the raft, though I have no doubt a lumberman or an Indian would have been highly amused at it. When the tide came in it floated, however, and the nine of us got on to it and poled it out from the shore, trying to keep as close in as possible. Unfortunately I had given the Eskimos some tobacco, in order to get them to go with me, and as soon as we were afloat they thought it would be a good time for a smoke, and all sat down and lit their pipes. With no one but myself poling, we began to spin round and round, and, getting into cross-currents, we gradually drifted into deep water, where I could not reach the bottom. The Eskimos continued to smoke in spite of all I could say, and soon we were getting well out into the middle of the river, and were going down instead of up. It looked very much as if we might go right out to sea. Fortunately some of the fort men saw our danger, told Mr. Spencer, and he sent out a boat which towed us in to land. As soon as we landed and had made the raft fast, the Eskimos jumped ashore, and said they must at once leave for the north. I tried hard to get them to help me carry up the lumber, but nothing would induce them to stay. However, I had now got all the lumber on hand, and set to work to carry and drag it up to the site.

When I came to lay the foundation of the house, I was at a loss to know just how to go about it, being absolutely without any experience of this kind of work. Still, " necessity is the mother of invention," and my necessity was great enough, in all conscience. I knew, even then, that we could never live through the coming winter in that little iron church. We should simply freeze to death, and there was no other place available.

Fortunately, at this juncture, the *Alert* returned to Churchill for a stay of some days, as they had to make up some charts, which could not well be done at sea. Commander Gordon very kindly offered to lend me three men who had some knowledge of building. They could only give me two days, but were willing to work as long as they could see. As a result of two very long days' work we put together the framework of the house, but on the 20th of August the *Alert* had to leave, and I was deprived of the assistance of my expert workmen. We owe a very great debt of gratitude to Commander Gordon and Dr. R. Bell, without whose encouragement and support the Mission on the western shores of the Bay might, and without doubt would, have been delayed for years, if not given up altogether.

After the departure of the *Alert*, I continued to work as hard as possible on the building, sometimes even from fourteen to sixteen hours a day. More than once I was in despair and almost inclined to give in, but my wife would come and hold the boards whilst I fitted them into place, and encouraged me in every possible way. Often I went to bed so tired out that I thought I would never be able to continue, but next morning I was up and at it again.

The long delay in the arrival of the Company's ship was also a cause of great anxiety at this time. Up to the end of August nothing had been seen or heard of her, and supplies were running very low indeed. Moreover, on the 4th of September we had one of the most furious gales I ever remember, and we felt quite sure that if the ship was anywhere near Churchill she must be in very grave danger.

About a week later a ship's boat arrived in the river with the mate of the *Cam Owen* and three men, from whom we learned that the ship had been wrecked on Cape Churchill. On the 4th of September she was becalmed in the Churchill Bight, almost within sight of the river, when all at once the gale came upon her, and in trying to work her way offshore, she struck two or three times on the cape. She began to leak so badly that the pumps could not keep the water down and the captain dared not go out to sea. As the only means of saving his passengers—there being no port for which he could make—he decided to run his vessel ashore and take his chances. This he did about twenty miles south of the cape.

The coast is very low and shallow, with reefs running all the way along several miles out from shore, and thanks to the abnormally high water at Churchill that night, the tide rose over twenty feet—being nearly eight feet above the normal—she was able to run right up to the beach, and at low water was left high and dry, so that the passengers and crew were able to walk ashore.

With two of the coast's boats Mr. Spencer, Mr. McTavish the clerk, and I at once started for the wreck to see if we could do anything to help them, and try to save some of the supplies we so greatly needed. They could not possibly leave, as they had only three small boats, and snow had fallen and the coast was lined with ice.

The Founding of the Churchill Mission

When we reached the wreck we found the whole party safely in camp on shore, including the Rev. G. S. and Mrs. Winter with their one child and a maid, also Dr. Milne, who was coming out as medical man for York.

A single glance at the vessel enabled us to realize what a terrible experience they must have had. It was obvious at once that the ship was damaged beyond all possibility of repair—in fact, it was a wonder that she had not gone to pieces on the reefs which fringe the coast, and on which she struck several times before reaching the beach. But for the very high tide she must have done this, and in all probability all hands must have been lost, for there was no one to help them on the shore.

It was decided to send on all the passengers and crew to York in one of the boats we had brought, and as soon as they got off we started to try and save what we could from the wreck. It was a most serious matter for us, since very little of last year's supplies remained at the post, and no other ship could possibly be expected before the following July or August.

Although one could walk out to the wreck at low water, at high tide she was submerged; consequently the greater part of the cargo was spoiled by the water, which was already beginning to freeze ship and cargo into one solid and immovable mass. We managed to save a small quantity of supplies, including a few barrels of damaged flour, with which we returned to Churchill, uncomfortably conscious of the hardships the coming winter had in store for us. Confident as we were of our ability to endure and to survive the approaching privations, we well knew that we should have to suffer the inconvenience of being without many things which even the poorest consider necessities.

All this naturally interfered greatly with my building operations. Ten days of the most precious time had been lost and winter was fast approaching. Already there was a foot of snow on the ground, and with the thermometer below zero work in the open was not altogether pleasant. However, by the middle of October we moved into a structure of four walls and a roof, which I had managed to put together. At the very sight of it anyone unaccustomed to life in the north would have thrown up his hands in horror and exclaimed at the impossibility of attempting to spend a winter in such a house. Yet it was a great improvement on the little iron church, for we could at any rate keep the temperature inside above freezing-point, a thing we had for weeks past been unable to accomplish in our recent abode.

Mr. R. Munro Ferguson, A.D.C. to Lord Aberdeen, spent some six weeks with us in 1894 in the little mission house, and from an amusing account he wrote of his experiences I append the following extract descriptive of our life at this time: " The missionary strains every nerve and works with superhuman endurance, sawing the timbers to refit them into place, and hammering nails like one who means to die hard, for he would freeze in his light, draughty, leaky iron church when it came to be forty or fifty below zero. To hold services, by the way, in this little church, all the furniture had usually to be piled on the bed, and much disinfecting powder employed after a score or two of Indians and Eskimos had been huddled together in the interior. Just before the first pinch of the fast-coming arctic winter, the rough outline of the house is finished—two rooms, or three, with a partition, all in rough boarding, with only high walls outside—but it was a shelter, and their own home; though most of it was still to be made. They lived there that winter airily; the single windows would freeze over with such a thick coating of frost that they adopted the method of ironing them with a hot iron to let daylight in again. The thermometer in very cold weather would sink to perhaps thirty below zero inside their single-boarded house, and getting up in the morning to light the fires was no joke in such a temperature, unless one happened to be an Eskimo or an Indian."

To people living in England, or even in the civilized parts of Canada, this account may seem to be very much overdrawn, but to its absolute accuracy both my wife and I can testify.

CHAPTER VIII

OLD FORT PRINCE OF WALES AND CHURCHILL TRADING POST

AT the mouth of the Churchill River, as it empties itself into Hudson's Bay, on a high sand ridge overlooking the Bay on two sides and guarding the entrance of the river, stands one of the largest and most massive ruins on the North American Continent, scarcely inferior in any detail to Louisbourg or to Old Quebec.

This fort was constructed by the Hudson's Bay Company, but is now the property of the Canadian Government. It is built of solid stone, with walls 20 feet high and 20 feet wide at the top, strengthened by four bastions at each of the four corners. Forty-two cannon, of the largest and heaviest calibre of the age, mounted on the walls rendered the task of forcing an entry into the river practically impossible. No hostile warship of the time could have passed through the narrow entrance, at this point but little more than a quarter of a mile wide, for the fort lies close to the river bank, and on the opposite shore stands a battery also equipped with heavy guns.

The fortifications were commenced in 1733, and

are said to have taken twenty years to build, but this is a very doubtful statement. Within the fort were storehouses, powder magazine, dwelling houses and offices, all of stone.

Joseph Robson, the surveyor and builder, was brought out from England for this purpose: he describes one of the buildings inside the fort as being 101 feet long, 33 feet wide, and 17 feet high, with leaded roof.

For many years the chief factor in charge of Fort Churchill was Samuel Hearne, the well-known arctic explorer. He made two expeditions into the north country in 1769 and 1770, but was driven back each time by lack of provisions, or by the desertion of the Indians with whom he was travelling, but in 1772 he succeeded in making his way across country, with a large band of Chipewyan Indians, to the mouth of the Coppermine River. Here the Indians fell in with a small party of Eskimos and massacred every one of them. Hearne was unable to protect them, as he was in fear of the Indians. Thus, for the first time, the mysteries of the hitherto unknown arctic coasts were penetrated.

Ten years later, in 1782, whilst Hearne was still in charge of Fort Churchill, three French men-of-war under Admiral La Perouse appeared in Hudson's Bay and anchored off the fort. On the following day La Perouse landed 400 men and summoned the fort to surrender. Hearne seems to have capitu-

lated without attempting to strike a blow in its
defence: possibly he argued that he was not a
soldier fighting for the defence of his country, but
a " rat-catcher " working for the good of a fur
company.

For two days the French soldiers tried to demolish
the fort, but were unable to do much more than
spike and dismantle the guns, overthrow the top
row of the massive granite stones, and blow up
a small part of the western side and the gateway
with its stone outworks.

Samuel Hearne was carried off to France as a
prisoner-of-war, doubtless together with all the furs
he had managed to gather together for the Company.
Thus " Old Fort Prince of Wales," the pride of the
north country, was left a deserted ruin: yet it still
stands in much the same condition as that in which
La Perouse left it in 1782.

After the capture of Fort Prince of Wales, the
Company made no attempt to rebuild, but sent in
a bill to the British Government for some thousands
of pounds for failing to protect their factory at
Churchill. This was paid, I believe, by the French
Government. Then the Company built a small
wooden fort on the site of the present trading post,
5 miles up the river.

This post is situated on the shore of a small bay,
well sheltered from the north by the high ridge
of rocks which separate the Churchill River from
Button's Bay. The river opposite the fort is nearly

five miles wide, but, as the channel at low water
is less than one mile, the boulder-strewn mud-flats
prevent the approach of any boat except at high
tide.

When I first visited Churchill in 1884 portions of
the stockade of the fort were still standing, but now
these have all disappeared, and there is no sign
whatever of any fort.

The winter is, of course, very long and very severe
at Churchill, and the snowfall heavy. According to
meteorological records Churchill is, I believe, the
coldest place in Canada, taking the mean of the
three winter months.

Whilst the stockades remained they were usually
completely covered with snow to the depth of 8 or
10 feet; through these snow-banks it was a common
thing to cut tunnels and pathways to the various
houses and stores, so that often the master did not
have to go out into the open to get from one place
to another. Many of the houses would be quite
buried, and had to be dug out two or three times
during the winter. Now the palisades have all
been removed, and with them the high snow-drifts
have disappeared.

The seasons of the year differ greatly from those
of Southern Canada, or even from the climate
south in James's Bay. It was frequently said that
at Churchill we had only two seasons, " nine months'
winter, and three months' bad weather," but I have

also heard another description, which fits equally well: " Nine months' winter, and three months' flies."

Summer and winter follow each other so closely that spring and autumn can scarcely be said to exist. By the middle of October the marshes are always frozen over, and usually the whole country is covered with snow, sometimes to the depth of a foot or more. The river generally becomes ice-bound by the end of October, though one may not be able to cross before the middle or end of November. Once frozen, even the spring tides, which often rise to a height of 14 or 16 feet, have no effect on the ice, which is often 6 or more feet thick. Not until mid-June can the sun compel the frost to relax its hold. The average date of the opening of the river for some ten years was the 20th of June, but the ice often floats in and out of the river up to the middle of July, and snow-banks may be seen even in August.

Myriads of mosquitoes and black flies plague the luckless inhabitants throughout the short summer. In no place in the world are mosquitoes worse than on the western shores of Hudson's Bay, and at Churchill in particular.

In 1884, when the Hudson's Bay ship had to winter at Churchill, the mate, an old salt who had been in nearly all known parts of the world, would not believe that mosquitoes could be bad in such a cold country. The following July, when they began to get their ship out of her winter quarters, he would not be persuaded to wear gloves and veil, as even the natives are obliged to do, but went down to the ship without any such protection, saying he was not an old woman, and knew what mosquitoes were. It was murky weather and a lovely day for flies. The old man worked on for a time wiping the flies off in handfuls, but at last he could stand it no longer, and throwing down his spade, with some very strong language, he made tracks for the fort, two miles away, as fast as he could go; the first thing he did was to go into the store and buy gloves and a veil, saying he thought he knew what flies were, but he had never seen any so bloodthirsty as this lot.

One writer declares that " they (the mosquitoes) crowd in such numbers at Churchill as to crush one another to death, and the victims lie sometimes in such heaps that they have to be swept out twice a day. Nothing but the north-east or the north-west wind, bringing with it the chill of the ice-fields, gives relief from these tormentors." There is a certain amount of humorous exaggeration in this account, but it can safely be asserted that no description adequately represents the annoyance and irritation caused by these pests of the northern summer.

As I have already said, the country in the neighbourhood of Churchill is very rocky and almost treeless. In consequence of this firewood is very difficult to get anywhere near the place. A plentiful supply can be obtained some fifty miles inland, but this cannot be hauled home in winter, and the Churchill River is a very difficult one to get a raft down.

Attempts have been made to raise vegetables, but with very poor results. A few turnips and lettuces have been grown, but potatoes and other root crops are out of the question; they cannot be put into the ground before June, and any time in July they may be frozen. It is my firm conviction that no land within 100 miles of Churchill could be farmed or used for grazing purposes with any prospect of success.

But the landscape is by no means bleak and colourless during the short summer. The whole country seems to be covered with wild flowers, which spring up quickly, and almost as quickly die away. Between thirty and forty specimens of arctic flowers were gathered in one season by my daughter, and Mrs. Moody, of the Royal North-West Mounted Police, collected many more.

CHAPTER IX

THE work of the Mission at Churchill progressed
quietly and steadily. In addition to the Eskimos
and Indians, there were about sixty English-speaking
people at the fort. The natives stayed at the post
or in its neighbourhood only during the short
summer; in the winter they were scattered throughout the surrounding country for hundreds of miles,
supported entirely by their hunting and fishing,
this being the only way of making a living in the
north country.

The missionary was expected to be able to extract
teeth, to set, and even to amputate, limbs, and to
prescribe remedies for all the ills to which the flesh
is heir. Not only was he a medical practitioner as
well as a missionary, but he had also to act as his
own joiner, builder, blacksmith, bricklayer, mason,
or other skilled workman. Then again he was often
called upon to visit a sick Indian or Eskimo a
hundred miles away, which entailed a long and
trying walk on snow-shoes and an absence of many
days or even weeks.

I well remember on one occasion paying a short

visit to some Indians staying about thirty miles north of Churchill. Although we were then in the middle of May, everything was still frozen solid. After walking across Button's Bay, over very rough ice, for about four hours, we at last reached an Indian tent in which we found a man, his wife, two daughters, and a son-in-law.

Ten days before, when they had left the post, the old woman, who had only one eye, was suffering terribly from snow-blindness, and I had given her some lotion. I now found her sitting at the back of the tent moaning with pain, and her eye bound up. Upon taking off this bandage to examine her eye, I was horrified to find the eyeball oozing from its socket. When I asked her for an explanation of this she very quietly replied, " Oh, Yalty (minister), the pain was so great, I got my daughter Aggie to cut it in order to let out some of the pain." This her daughter had done with a pair of scissors. My anger and amazement may be imagined. The poor old soul was now totally blind, and being very feeble was entirely dependent upon her family. There was really nothing to be done, the eye was gone and could not be replaced; all that one could do was to get the eyeball out and let the wound heal. Some years after I discovered that this same woman had lost the other eye in exactly the same way. I was very glad she did not tell me at the time, or I think I should hardly have known what to do. Snow-blindness is certainly one of the most painful things

I know, but the insane folly of this barbarous act is almost incredible, yet I can vouch for its truth.

I determined to stay the night with these Indians, not that I could do anything for the poor woman: that was past the skill of man. We were encamped right down upon the seashore, without any shelter except an Indian tent. During the night a very severe gale came on, and it snowed for all it was worth; next morning the snow had drifted so much into the tent that we were all buried under it. A frightful blizzard was raging so that we could not venture out, and as usual with Indians there was hardly a stick of firewood, and none to be got within less than two miles; this was by no means the worst, for there was hardly a bite of anything to eat. Indians always live a very happy-go-lucky, hand-to-mouth existence when out hunting. My own supply of food was intended to last me for about a week, but it did not go far amongst so large a party: the gale continued for two whole days, and we dared not go out. I cannot recollect two more miserable days in my life.

On the third day the snow ceased, and as we had nothing at all to eat, I set out to visit the Indians who had asked me to come; they were encamped about ten miles farther up the coast. I started without anything more solid than a cup of tea, and the walking was very heavy. When I reached the camp I found all the Indians in pretty much the same state as we had been; they had not been able to hunt, consequently the cupboard was bare. In going round the tents I found one man who had shot a goose that morning, and when I told them I had nothing to eat before starting that morning, they at once set to work to cook the goose, and I had my first meal for twenty-four hours. It was only, as we say in the north, " goose straight "—that is, " goose boiled in white water," without condiments, dressing, etc., and eaten without either vegetables, bread, or anything—but I enjoyed that goose far better than many served up with all the elaborate dressings of civilization. Truly " hunger is the best sauce."

After spending the day in visiting the tents and holding service I returned in the evening to the blind woman's tent, as by so doing I hoped to meet with other Indians from still farther north. When I got back I found that the two men had been out all day in their " goose stands," but had got nothing; consequently, after prayers and a drink of tea, we went supperless to bed, in the hope that next day would bring better luck.

In the morning the men were up and off by daylight, but returned about eight o'clock with nothing, and we breakfasted upon prayers and coffee. This scanty meal over, and prospects not looking very bright, I decided to make tracks for home: the people begged me to stay, as they would be sure to get something to eat during the day. As the other Indians had not turned up I thought I had better depart, so about ten o'clock I started out for my 20-mile walk. It was a day to be remembered, beautifully fine, and so warm that the snow melted, and I had to plough through slush and water. I became quite played out, and had to lie down many times to rest on the wet snow.

I reached home late that night utterly exhausted; for thirty hours I had been without food, and in that time had walked through untrodden snow and slush for 30 miles. This is not at all an uncommon thing for an Indian, but whatever it may be to him, it was by no means a pleasant thing to me.

The absence of a medical man was felt severely at times, though, as a rule, the health of the place was very good. The nearest doctor was at York Factory, 200 miles away. There was not a single death during our first two years at Churchill; still, the knowledge was ever present that in the event of serious illness professional assistance was impossible.

I did what I could with my small medicine chest, but a qualified doctor was undoubtedly a necessity. The following spring the birth of our only child took place, and there was neither doctor nor nurse to be had, the missionary as usual being both; my wife's health became far from satisfactory, and, as her case baffled such medical skill as I possessed, I sent a message twice asking the doctor to come on to Churchill, but for some reason he failed to appear, although there were two chances for him to do so.

A Thousand Miles from a Post Office

We waited until the following December, and then, two Indians having come on from York Factory, I determined to go and see the doctor in person.

We started on the 6th of December, in fine but bitterly cold weather; of course, we had to tramp, as I could not spare my dogs—they were needed to keep the fires going. As luck would have it, the Indians lost their way, and we wandered many miles out of our course. It is often said that an Indian is never lost and this is true in a sense, for they generally reach their destination in the end; but it frequently happens that an Indian will wander about for hours, and even for days, before arriving at his journey's end, yet he rightly tells you he is not lost, but merely gone astray. I remember one Indian I knew who, when met thus wandering about, and asked if he were lost, replied, " No, me no lost, wigwam lost."

Owing to a severe gale and the heavy snow, we were detained in one spot for two days, completely buried by the whirling blizzard, sheltered only by our blankets, and in a most miserable condition. When we reached the Nelson River we found it still open, and this meant a heavy tramp up the north shore, until we found the river frozen and could cross, and then down the south shore again until we were opposite York Factory.

The journey occupied eleven days, almost twice as long as usual, and I was deeply thankful to find rest and a bed with my fellow-missionary and his family. I succeeded in persuading the doctor to return with me; he said he could not possibly walk, so I got a team of Indian dogs and drove him back.

Our journey of a week was not particularly pleasant, for it was bitterly cold and every one in the party was rather badly frozen. I remember well we spent Christmas Day on one of the large desolate plains which lie between the trading posts. I had been away for twenty-one days, and did not know in what state we might find my wife, but, thank God, she was keeping up fairly well.

The doctor examined her, and said he could do little or nothing, as she must have an operation which he would not perform there; she must go to England. This was not very cheering news, as there was no possibility of making a start for England until the annual ship came in August, and what might happen in nine months no one could say. In any circumstances, we could not hope to reach England before the end of October or even November.

Truly the north country does teach patience and fortitude.

CHAPTER X

THROUGHOUT the rest of the winter and spring my wife maintained her wonted cheerfulness, and was able to keep about although in very feeble health all the time. All our Indians and Eskimos came in as usual, and we had a very busy time, but our hearts and minds were to a large extent fixed upon the coming of the ship, and with it the hope of reaching surgical aid.

She did not reach Churchill until about the 20th of August, and we were glad to find an old friend of my wife's as captain. We set sail for home on the 24th, but had first to go on to York Factory, and, as on our wedding trip, fell in with very bad weather; we were some ten days beating up and down the coast, and my wife was very ill indeed; so much so, that when we did at last reach York, Captain B., although most kind and anxious to help, felt obliged to refuse to take my wife any further. He was of the opinion that as the vessel was altogether lacking in proper accommodation for an invalid, with a sixteen-months-old baby, Mrs. L. would never stand the strain, and he did not want to bury her at sea. We were obliged, therefore, to leave

80

the ship at York. The only alternative was to remain at York for the winter or take a journey of some six hundred miles by canoe to Winnipeg, and then overland to New York, an exceedingly risky undertaking at that time of the year, for with the approach of winter we were liable to be frozen in before we reached Winnipeg. In any case, the venture would tax to the utmost the endurance of my wife and child. There seemed to be no way out of the difficulty. We had been waiting nine months, and what the result of another wait of nine months might be no one could tell, and so we decided to run the risk and try to get through. We therefore hired a small flat-bottomed boat and four Indians and started out on the 14th of September, making our way by the usual canoe route up the Hayes, Fox, and Hill Rivers to Oxford House, which we reached in thirteen days. We were indeed thankful to enjoy a good night's rest in a bed, under a roof, after many days of travelling cooped up in a very small boat from 5 a.m. till dusk.

On the whole, the weather had been fine, but at times we had to push on through rain, hail, and snow. This bad weather, combined with sleeping in the woods, without much comfort, was not beneficial to my wife's health, but she kept up very well, and was always bright and happy.

Our men had to return from Oxford, and we got other Indians and a birchbark canoe, which was even smaller than our boat, and on the 5th of October we started for Norway House. For several days we travelled under wretched conditions, but were obliged to push on, and at last reached Norway House at the head of Lake Winnipeg. There was no steamer, and the only way of getting into Winnipeg was by taking a York boat, and, after resting some five days, we started. This last stage of our journey to civilization was by far the most arduous and exasperating. No man willingly puts out on Lake Winnipeg in an open boat in October, for the storms are generally constant and severe. If we could reach Beren's River we might possibly catch a small steamer there, and we pushed on with this hope, but spent six most trying days before we got there, only to find that the steamer had been in a few days before and would not call again. She had gone to the north end of the lake, and was to call at " Swampy Island " on her way back. This was some twenty miles out from Berens River, and we at once put out again with the hope of catching her. We had run into this harbour under a coming gale, and when we got back to the mouth of the river it was blowing so hard that we dared not face it. Our last hope seemed shattered, but as these gales on the lake frequently subside as rapidly as they arise, we put ashore on a small barren rock in the mouth of the river, so that we might be ready to cross if the gale did go down. It was no place even for a brief sojourn; there was scarcely a stick of wood on the islet, and no shelter from the wind, but in our anxiety to reach Swampy Island we determined to stay there.

For two days and nights we held out on that barren spot, without firewood, rain, sleet, and snow falling the whole time, so that we were nearly frozen. At the end of the second day we were forced to abandon our position, and run before the gale to the mainland for shelter and a fire, as there seemed little or no hope of our getting much further on our journey. During that night the gale began to go down, and in the early morning the lake was almost calm. At 3 a.m. on a cold, clear morning with bright moonlight we put out for "Swampy." The only settlement on the island was a small fishing station, and we had no idea where it was situated. As the island is 20 miles long, we expected some difficulty in finding the shanties. The moon went down, and it was pitch dark when we at last struck the island; it had taken us six hours to cross. The water froze on our oars, and my wife and child suffered greatly from the cold. At last, shortly after daylight, we sighted the fishing station, and at once knew the steamer had not been in yet, for we saw Mr. J. W. McLean (" Big Bear ") standing on the jetty. He had crossed from Berens River some days before us in order to catch the steamer, which had promised to call there for him. Much of our pain and suffering was at once forgotten, for there was still a prospect of getting into Winnipeg.

Our Indians were most anxious to get back to

A Thousand Miles from a Post Office

Norway House, and would not even land to have a cup of tea, a most unusual thing for them; the weather was so threatening, however, that they were afraid of being frozen in before they could reach home.

The only habitable building on the island was a large fish refrigerator from which all the ice had been removed, and some degree of comfort was supplied by a small cooking-stove. For this we were indebted to Mr. McLean and two or three fishing men, who were stranded there like ourselves.

In this refrigerator, where privacy was out of the question, we lived for three days, and it seemed as if we should have to stay there until the lake froze over, which would not be much before Christmas. Snow fell every day, and the ground was covered to the depth of more than a foot.

We had no food, but fortunately one of the men had some potatoes, and we managed to get fish from the lake, although it was the close season. On the morning of our fourth day the steamer hove in sight, and we rejoiced greatly at the thought of release. She had been detained by the gale, so what had seemed a trial, as is often the case, turned out to be a blessing. The day after leaving Swampy we landed in Selkirk, and we felt that now we had reached civilization all our trials were practically over. We spent two days there resting, and then went into Winnipeg, and took the night train for New York, without troubling to visit Niagara Falls on the way, and on the 30th of October embarked on board the *Arizona*, and landed in England on the 8th of November, having taken almost three months in travelling the 7,000 miles.

Only those who have been through a similar experience can form any idea of the strain this journey had been to us all, more especially to my wife, who endured the hardships we had undergone with the greatest fortitude. Our little daughter was extremely ill in crossing the Atlantic, so much so that for some days she hung between life and death; but, thank God, she was restored to complete health when we finally reached home.

Immediately upon our arrival in England, early in November, my wife was placed in the hands of a surgeon, by whose skill a completely successful operation was performed; but her health greatly suffered, so that when I arranged to return—at the end of seven months' vacation chiefly spent in deputation work for the Church Missionary Society, and in raising money for a new church, which we greatly needed for our mission station—I suggested that she should remain behind and rejoin me in the following year. This plan she would not consent to, and it was finally decided that we should all return together in the summer.

On the 21st of June, therefore, we left our home to join the Hudson's Bay Company's sailing vessel at Stromness. We stayed for an hour in Edinburgh, and also in Perth, and spent the night in Inverness, where we had an opportunity of admiring the lovely situation of the Highland capital. From Inverness we enjoyed the magnificent scenery along the route of the East Coast Railway, and the night boat from Thurso landed us in Stromness in the early hours of the morning.

The next ten days were spent in visiting places of interest in the neighbourhood of the quaint old town; for though our vessel, the *Prince Rupert*, of 500 tons, had come into the harbour two days before we arrived, she had to wait for her sister ship, the *Lady Head*, bound for Moose Fort, which had not yet reached the harbour.

On the 3rd of July we sailed away from Stromness, passing through Hoy Sound into the Northern Atlantic, where we got a splendid view of Rona, a lofty precipitous rock on which only a few sheep and innumerable gulls could be seen. The latter, when disturbed, gave quite a snowy appearance to the cliffs.

Whilst running close under the south coast of Greenland, on our twelfth day at sea, we encountered a heavy gale, which carried away some thirty feet of the ship's railing. Fortunately no other damage was done. Cape Chidley, the southern headland, rose up before us at the entrance of Hudson's Strait like a grim sentinel of the desolate northern fastnesses.

We soon found ourselves surrounded by numerous icebergs of all shapes and sizes: I counted no less than forty enormous bergs in plain sight on one occasion. The ice crunched and ground against the vessel's sides with a menacing sound, calculated to terrify the inexperienced arctic voyager.

About forty miles up the Strait, a thick fog enveloped us, through which nothing was visible 100 yards away, and for three days we were anchored to ice-floes. When at last it lifted and we were able to take our bearings, we found that we were some twenty miles outside the Strait, having drifted with the ice some sixty miles. We considered ourselves very fortunate not to have struck any of the many rocks to the south of the Strait. It took us nearly a month to work our way through the Strait into Hudson's Bay. On the way we had a magnificent view of Grinnell's Glacier, which we could quite plainly see with the glasses sparkling in the sun, though 50 miles away.

On the 22nd of August, after a splendid run across the Bay, we sighted the rocks of the Churchill River, and at midday were safely at anchor in the snug little harbour, within 5 miles of our little wooden shanty, having been just fifty days on the voyage out from Stromness. We had been away a year all but four days. Everything was just as we had left it; our house had remained closed and undisturbed, and the same familiar faces greeted us delightedly as we landed.

During our short stay in England I had succeeded in raising £200, with which we had purchased a small iron church, but the Hudson's Bay Company were not able to bring it out that year, and we had still to occupy the old dilapidated church in summer, using our house for all services during the winter and also for day-school.

Most of the Eskimos and Indians had left for their northern hunting-grounds before our arrival, only a few of the Chipewyans staying behind to welcome us back amongst them.

CHAPTER XI

THE CHIPEWYAN INDIAN OF THE NORTH

THE " Chips," as we somewhat disrespectfully term
them, are the most northerly of the Indians found
on Hudson's Bay, and seldom come south of Cape
Churchill.   They are a peculiarly sullen and reserved
race, much more so than the Crees or Ojibways.
Any feeling or expression of gratitude is foreign
to their nature, and of the gentle amenities and
gracious courtesies of social intercourse they are
absolutely ignorant.   Their language, indeed, seems
even to lack the commonest phrases of appreciation
or thanks.

This aloofness and stolid indifference made the
task of winning their confidence exceedingly difficult, and my wife and I doubted at first whether
we should ever succeed in gaining their trust and
friendship.   It was not until we began to care for
some of their sick in our own home that we discovered very warm hearts and feelings beneath
their impassive demeanour.

I have seen it stated that " the Chipewyan Indian
is naturally the roughest, harshest savage to be
found on the Continent; his disposition is sullen
and morose."   On first coming into contact with

him I heartily concurred with this view: it is the
impression invariably received from a first super-
ficial acquaintance with the race. But this un-
attractive characteristic is, I believe, largely the
result of the rough hand-to-mouth existence which
they lead; the stern battle of life is fought under
conditions which tend to wipe out all emotional
display. A stolid immobility of expression and
character is the natural outcome of their perpetual
conflict with the forces of Nature. When one
comes to know them better they display many
points of interest: their characters exhibit traces
of a simple nobility not always found in more
favoured races.

An enormous stretch of country was at one time
peopled by Indians of the Chipewyan stock. The
extent of this expansion is concisely described by
Butler in his " Wild West." He says: " The
Chipewyans are found at Churchill on Hudson's
Bay and at Fort Simpson on the rugged coast of
New Caledonia; but, stranger still, far down in
Arizona and Mexico, even as far south as Nicaragua,
the guttural language of the Chipewyan race is still
heard, and the wild Navajos and fierce Apache
horsemen of the Mexican plains are akin to the
fur-hunters of the north. Of the many ramifica-
tions of the Indian race this perhaps is the most
extraordinary.

" To the east of the Rocky Mountains these races
call themselves ' Tinne ' (at Churchill, ' Dinna '),

The Chipewyan Indian of the North

a name which signifies ' people,' with that sublimity of ignorance which makes most savage people imagine themselves the sole proprietors of the earth. Many subdivisions exist amongst them; these are the Copper Indians and Dog Ribs of the Barren Grounds; the Louchen or Kutchins, a fierce tribe of the Upper Yukon; the Yellow Knives, Hares, Nahanies, and Sickanies, of the Great Slave Lake; the Chipewyans of Athabasca and Portage la Roche; and the Beavers of the Peace River.

" West of the Rocky Mountains the Carriers, still a branch of the Chipewyan stock, intermingle with the numerous Atnah races of the coast. On the North Saskatchewan a small wild tribe called Surcees also spring from this great family, and, as we have said, nearly three thousand miles away, far down on the tropic plains of Old Mexico, the stuttering ' tch ' accent grates upon the ear. Spread over such a vast extent of country it may well be supposed that they vary very much in physiognomy."

Many curious legends are current amongst them, several of which I collected at various times during my residence amongst them at Churchill. As in the myths of many other savage races there is a rather bewildering inconsequence of incident in these stories, most of which derive their origin from the evolutions and phenomena of Nature. The mythologist and antiquary could doubtless trace to a common source the inner signification of many of these stories. I give the following fragmentary tale as a specimen:

" In the beginning there were no men; but the animals resembled men in that they could speak. When they possessed the power of speech it was summer, and winter when they lost it. A squirrel foretold the coming of winter, whereupon they all began to cry. Then they ascended into the sky to meet an all-powerful being who dwelt there, by whom they were ordered to return again to the earth. He informed them further that his son was upon the earth ' to watch the deer crossing the river.'

" Now the mysterious person who watched the river told a mouse that when the deer appeared he would go out in a canoe and kill some of them. The deer, becoming acquainted with these evil intentions, said to the mouse, ' When you see the evil-minded slayer coming in his canoe do you swim out and bite his paddle in the middle so that he may upset before he reaches us.' The mouse did so and the canoe upset, but the occupant succeeded in gaining the shore.

"A bag was found by the deer in the canoe, and it contained summer. Thereupon they followed the man-spirit to a certain place from which they could see his father in the sky. When they had all ascended into the sky again the bag was opened, and out tumbled all kinds of fish. A jack-fish came forth first, and under his leadership all the fish and animals set out to find the earth again. The fissure through which they made their exit from the sky seemed to close up behind them.

" Whilst they were still in search of the earth, and just before they found it, a second partition of the bag burst open, thereby letting out summer or heat. The snow, which at that time covered the earth, immediately melted and the land became flooded, except on one spot, whereon they beheld another man-like being. At their request he drank up the water and saved them from the flood. But there was now no water to be found anywhere.

" Thereupon a lynx came to him and said, ' My grandfather, the earth is now so dry that neither I nor any of the animals can travel on it for want of water: we shall die of thirst. Tell me where you have put all the water.' Upon learning that he had drunk it the lynx obtained permission to place a pan upon the part of his body where the water lay. At once it began to flow over the earth again in rivers, the courses of which were traced by the swallower with his staff.

" Being now without food the animals began to die of starvation, and especially the deer. Summer-hawks were to be seen watching for the deer, whose presence was indicated by the number of crows hovering over them. The wolves, foxes, and other animals which prey upon the deer also took advantage of this sign, but many of them died before they came up with the deer. When the remainder arrived they discovered that a partition made from the tripe and inner fat of the deer separated them from their prey, but a whiskey-jack picked a hole in it and brought out some fat for his friends. The lynx then poked his nose through the opening and received such a blow from a deer that he has had a short dinted snout ever since. Soon afterwards the deer issued forth from their refuge and spread over the earth. All these events happened before the creation of man."

CHAPTER XII

DURING the winter of 1887 the work of the Mission at Churchill seemed to make very satisfactory progress. The people of the fort encouraged and aided us most willingly, and the Eskimos and Indians in their periodic visits to the trading post evinced a real genuine desire to learn more and more about the loving-kindness of the great and good Father, in whom they unconsciously believed.

Their standard of bodily cleanliness, in spite of marked improvement, was, however, still so far from perfect that their presence for service in our little three-roomed house was not altogether an unmixed blessing. The only way we could at all stand it was to get there first, and gradually become accustomed to the rank atmosphere. Then, as soon as service was over, we opened the windows and rushed outside; we could not stay out long, for in winter, even if the thermometer was up to sixty in the house, with the windows open it would drop down to freezing-point in about five minutes.

Consequently we hailed with joy the arrival of the ship in August, 1890, for she had on board the iron church purchased in England the previous year.

95

The task of unloading the mass of timber and iron from the ship, which was anchored 5 miles away from the Mission, was no light one, but by the end of the month I was in a position to begin the construction of the building. Of course, all the material had been cut and fitted in England; nevertheless, the putting together of such a building, measuring 50 feet by 25 feet, was hard work for one man.

Unfortunately, one day in September, when the outside was rapidly nearing completion, and I was at work on the chancel, I lost my footing and fell a distance of 12 feet on to the floor beams, seriously fracturing two of my ribs and shaking me up terribly. With the assistance of a boy of twelve, who happened to be with me, I managed to crawl to the house, where my wife bound up my injuries as well as she was able. There was no hope of obtaining the help of a doctor, as even the journey of 200 miles to York Factory was impossible at that time of the year.

I had to remain in bed for ten days, fretting and fuming at the enforced suspension of my work, for the state of the church was such that the whole building would probably be carried away once the winter gales began. It was most difficult to practise the patience and resignation so easily preached. At the end of ten days I was back again at work on the church, though scarcely able to walk, but there was no one else to turn to, and I was most anxious to finish the outside and shut it up, so that it would not be blown away during the winter. Naturally I suffered a good deal from my injured ribs during this hard work, but it is wonderful what one can stand when there is no way out. The autumn was very mild, and by the end of October I had so far completed the building that I could suspend operations on it for the winter without any misgivings for its safety. We had no stove to heat the church with, and even if we had had, it would have been no use, for it would have taken me all my time to haul firewood for it, so work had to stop.

It is a common saying that misfortunes never come singly, and in our case the second misfortune threatened at one time to be most serious.

On the 21st of November one of the terrible winter gales so frequent at Churchill came upon us with most savage fury. Our Indian boy was on his way down to the house one evening during the gale, and when passing the church he was nearly knocked over by a board torn from the church roof. Looking up he discovered that half of one side of the roof had disappeared, and came and told us of this. Donning my Eskimo costume I fought my way through the storm to inspect the extent of the disaster, and found one of the doors had been burst open by the gale and about twenty feet of one side of the roof nowhere to be seen—it had evidently been carried away on to the river some quarter of a mile away; the other half of the same side had slipped down about a foot, but still remained on the building. Assistance was hurriedly obtained from the fort, and for two hours we worked in that blinding gale, and anchor-chains and ropes were passed over the roof to keep it in place if possible. There was nothing else that could be done, and I then returned dejected and disconsolate to my wife, for it appeared highly probable that the whole church might be swept away before morning.

We had passed through deep waters together before, but that night we felt completely overwhelmed, and for a time we sat and wept in despair. Then we remembered that we had a Father, who never laid upon His children more than they could carry, and had promised grace and strength to those who ask it, and we prayed that night, I think, as we never prayed before.

The gale raged with unexampled fury for two days and nights, during which we could do nothing but look on helplessly, and yet hopefully, now we had cast the burden on to the Lord. Our prayers were undoubtedly answered, for the church emerged triumphantly from the ordeal, and a week of exceptionally mild weather followed which enabled us to repair the damage inflicted by the storm. Mr. Spencer, who had kept a very careful record of the weather during his twenty years' residence at Churchill, assured us that he had never known such a mild spell at that time of the year. The thermometer rose to just about freezing-point, and the days were bright and calm.

The Building of a Church in the North

We discovered the missing portion of the roof on the river, nearly a quarter of a mile away. It was, of course, badly broken, but with the aid of some of the men I was able to replace it in position, and the church was once more intact. We took every possible precaution to prevent any of the doors or windows from blowing open again. Throughout that winter the building stood firm and safe, and it has weathered many a storm since then.

During the ensuing spring and summer the work of construction was steadily pushed forward, but as I had to do all the work alone it was not until the summer of 1892 that the church was formally opened for divine service.

This building is still standing at Churchill, reverenced and beloved by many an Indian and Eskimo, as well as by the white population of the fort. When Bishop Newnham of Moosonee visited us in 1895 he complimented us by saying that it was the most complete, comfortable, churchlike building in the whole Diocese of Moosonee, a tribute to our handiwork which made us feel that our labour, even in its material aspect, had not been in vain, apart from the great spiritual awakening amongst the natives which the possession of such a place of worship helped to bring about. Many a poor soul has found peace and consolation within its walls.

CHAPTER XIII

SHETHNĀNEĀI, OR "THE BIG HILL," AND YORK FACTORY

AFTER the work on the church was finished, at least for that winter, I resumed the usual work of the Mission: the services, classes, and day-school were held in our little mission house, which measured only 23 feet by 19 feet, divided into just three rooms for all purposes.

One room was 19 feet long by 9 feet wide, and in this we had sometimes as many as fifty people, and as it was winter, when we were obliged to keep up big fires, it sometimes got so close that one could scarcely breathe.

For exercise and recreation I shot ptarmigan, on which we to a very large extent depended for animal food. In former years up to 1882 deer had been so abundant at Churchill that they used to run around about the place like rabbits, but that year there were some terrible fires around, all the moss was burnt up, and the deer left the region altogether. During my eighteen years at Churchill I only once saw a band of deer near the place, but since 1900 they have returned, the moss having grown up again, and there is never any difficulty in getting all the meat required.

Ptarmigan, like the rabbit of the north, is very poor food, especially in winter; there seems to be no nutriment in them; they manage to pick up just sufficient food to keep them alive and that is all. I have known whole families of Indians starve even when they had abundance of rabbits or ptarmigan, but having no fatty matter of any kind, or grain food, they would gradually pine away and die. The people would often come to us and tell us they were starving, having nothing but " ptarmigan boiled in white water "—that is, they had no pork or grease of any kind to mix with them.

Early in February that winter I started out to pay a long promised visit to a place called Shethnāneāi, or the " Big Hill," about one hundred and fifty miles west of Churchill. This is the place where the Indians often gather in winter, as there is good fishing in the large lake, and generally good hunting in the surrounding country. By joining some of the Hudson's Bay Company's men, who were going there for the purpose of trading furs, and had a good team of dogs, I avoided the necessity of hauling my own supplies, but there was no chance of riding, for our sledge was too heavy.

The first stage of the journey, across Button's Bay, was intensely disagreeable, as the thermometer showed thirty below zero, and a strong wind was blowing right in our faces. When we reached the woods on the other side and got into Seal River it was much better, and we pushed on until 5 p.m. and then prepared to camp for the night.

Camping when travelling in the north is the most unpleasant part of the day's work, but it is unavoidable, for there are no houses or stopping places of any kind. A favourable spot is selected where the trees are thickest, then the snow is dug away with the snow-shoes until one gets to the earth. Trees are then felled and arranged to form a wind-screen on three sides of the camp, the ground is strewn with pine-brush, a fire, as large as the supply of wood will allow (this is generally very small in the north of Canada), is built on the fourth side, and one's shelter is complete for the night.

After supper and prayers each man rolls himself up in his deerskin or rabbitskin robe (the latter is by far the best), and seeks what sleep the cold will permit him to enjoy. Should the night happen to be fine, the brilliancy of the stars and the sparkling and flashing of the Aurora Borealis will compensate him in some measure for his inability to sleep—I have often been able to read quite well at midnight simply by the light of this wonderful phenomenon of the north country—but in stormy weather, when shelter is poor and wood scarce, and one of the terrible blizzards is blowing, he tosses fretfully and uncomfortably for hours, and probably wakes up in the morning to find nearly a foot of snow covering blankets and everything else. At such times a large blazing fire is " a consummation devoutly to be wished for," and a wish it too often has to remain.

My feet were very badly blistered by my snow-shoes when we reached Shethnāneāi on the sixth day, and I was very glad to be at the end of my journey, where I could rest for a little time. We found only fourteen Indians encamped on the lake, the majority of them being about four days' journey farther west. I felt compelled to refuse a pressing request to go there, as there would be little possi-bility of an immediate return, and I had to get back within a short time. For three days we enjoyed some very hearty and pleasant services, and it was a treat to see the way in which the Indians entered into them. It would have shamed many a congre-gation gathered in some of the large, handsome, and comfortable buildings in which civilized Christians meet to worship God, or, too often, to worship them-selves. Then I again set my face homewards, where I arrived after another six days' tramp, having walked in all about three hundred and fifty miles to give these poor souls the opportunity of worship-ping God with their minister.

During the previous summer we had taken into our house a little Chipewyan girl, whose mother had treated her with great cruelty, having on one occasion broken her arm by throwing her out of the tent. As the woman was a poor widow with no one to look after her or hunt for her family, she made no objection to my sending the child to the Indian

A Thousand Miles from a Post Office

Home at Elkhorn, Manitoba. The duty of taking
the child to York, where she could meet the York
boats going south in June, naturally devolved upon
me; and so, being at home for about a month, I
started out on another tramp of 400 miles with York
as my destination.

On this trip I had the pleasure of the company of
Mr. John Spencer, the Hudson's Bay Company's
officer at Churchill, who had been unwell for some
time, and wished to consult the doctor at York
in regard to his health.

Favoured by excellent weather, we were able to
reach York in five days, and there I enjoyed the rare
joy and pleasure of spending nearly two weeks
in social intercourse with my fellow-missionary,
the Rev. G. S. Winter. The infrequency of these
meetings is one of the most keenly felt drawbacks
to life in the north. One is at times inclined to envy
those missionaries who are stationed in India, China,
or other places, where the comforts and even
luxuries of the homeland are at hand, not the least
of these being the society of one's fellow-country-
men. Our return journey was very far from
pleasant; the melting snow made walking and camping equally uncomfortable, and we were indeed
thankful to be able to make the journey in six days.

When summer came round our Eskimos and
Indians flocked to the post as usual; but the work of
the Mission was not destined to proceed without
interruption. Early in the season I received in-

formation from Bishop Horden, then Bishop of
Moosonee, that he was taking advantage of the sailing of a small vessel from Moose Factory to York to
pay a visit to the latter place. As he would not be
able to come so far north as Churchill, he asked me
to meet him if possible at York Factory. My wife
and I decided to go, taking with us our daughter and
maid, as we could not leave them alone.

A passage was secured in a boat bound for our
destination, an open boat without any accommodation, and in four days we were at York. We
took along with us our own small boat in which to
return, as there would be no other way of getting
back, so far as we knew.

We waited for some weeks at York till the
schooner from Moose turned up, but without the
Bishop. By some mischance he had missed her at
Fort George. Our journey had thus been in vain,
and there was no hope of seeing him. After we
had stayed with the Winters for nearly a month,
the annual ship arrived quite unexpectedly from
England. She had not been to Churchill, so the
captain very kindly offered us a passage, and we were
only too glad to accept, as going along the coast
in the *Mowbray Trotter*, a very small boat, would
not have been at all pleasant. This boat was given
to me for the Mission of Churchill by the late Canon
Mowbray Trotter of Gloucester. Unfortunately the
captain and crew were rather a rough lot, and they
had a great deal of drink on board, which they did

not spare, so that it was one of the roughest experiences I have ever had on the Bay.

It was by a mere chance we managed to reach Churchill, and I had to take the vessel into the harbour. As we ran into the river, an accident happened which might have cost the lives of several of the fort men; they came out to meet us, and, either owing to the strong tide or to mismanagement, got their boat right under the bows of the ship. The men had barely time to grasp the anchor chains and tackle when the boat went right under and came up at the stern; she then drifted ashore on the north side, and as she had very little in her at the time there was no great loss.

We were once more safe home, and deeply thankful, for that night a most terrible storm came on, and if we had followed the advice of some of the officers of the ship, who wanted us to anchor just outside the river, we must without doubt have been driven on to the rocks.

In connection with the work of the Mission, I had that year travelled fully twelve hundred miles either on my snow-shoes or in a small boat, but had the joy of knowing that something had been done to give the Gospel to these poor lost sheep of the northland.

CHAPTER XIV

MARBLE ISLAND

MARBLE ISLAND, so called on account of the very white granite rock of which it is composed, lies just south of Chesterfield Inlet, in the northern portion of Hudson's Bay, about five hundred miles north of Churchill.

In summer it, or rather the mainland opposite to it, is the meeting-place of the Eskimos from Bathurst Inlet, Repulse Bay, Cape Fullerton, and Baker Lake. As comparatively few of these Eskimos ever come so far south as Churchill, I was extremely anxious to visit them in their much-frequented camping-ground, but until the year 1892 the pressure of my work in summer had not permitted me to avail myself of the courtesy of the Hudson's Bay Company's officials, from whom I had a standing offer of a passage in the boats which were sent to the Island every year. In 1892, however, I had more time at my disposal, as most of my building was finished for the present, so I determined to go.

As fellow-travellers I had a clerk of the Company, one or two half-breeds, and over one hundred Eskimos, who had been camping during the spring and early summer at, or near, Old Fort Prince of Wales. We started on the 19th of July in two coast-boats, or small two-masted schooners. In one was a small cabin about six feet long and about four feet high; this was our only shelter, except such as could be formed by oil-cloths.

The first night out we anchored in the Churchill River, waiting for the Eskimos. I most sincerely hope never to spend such another night. Legions of mosquitoes made sleep entirely out of the question. Until we set sail next morning at 3.30 a.m. an unequal battle was waged against a small but intrepid foe whose numbers seemed to increase in proportion to the thousands we killed, and our tempers rose. Only by getting out to sea could we get rid of them and find any peace.

There are no harbours or havens of any sort on the western coast of the Bay for nearly five hundred miles north of Churchill. From the low shores long reefs run for miles out to sea, and the tide recedes so far that, unless the greatest care is exercised, one is apt to become stranded miles out to sea. With us, however, all went well until a heavy gale struck us on the fourth day out. Wind and sea combined to drive us on to the lee-shore, where the surf was breaking thunderously upon the rocks. We held on to our course as long as possible, but at length were compelled to drop our anchors and trust to them in the face of a gale blowing right across the 600 miles of the Bay. The strength of the anchors and cables alone saved us from being swept on to the reefs, with no hope of escape, for we were miles from the shore. In this perilous situation we remained for two days and nights, with the wind shrieking through the rigging, and the waves pounding on the hull. Both boats were in the same plight, in sight of each other, but quite unable to help one another.

After the gale had subsided a run of two days brought us to a large Eskimo encampment, where we were to part company from most of those who had travelled with us. As the boats could not approach close to the shore, the people had to disembark on rafts formed by lashing *kayaks*—or Eskimo boats—together. A comical sight it was to see men, women, children, dogs, tents, and household effects all tumbled and jumbled together on these ramshackle, frail-looking contrivances. One naturally feared a tragic sequel to the amusing scene, but every raft landed its composite cargo in safety When the whole party was on shore and the tents set up, the result was one of the largest Eskimo encampments I had ever seen in the north—there were fully one hundred and fifty of them.

Most of the Eskimos had travelled in one boat, not more than forty feet long. In this crowded space, adults, children, and dogs struggled for elbow room. I had intended travelling with the Eskimos, on purpose to be able to teach them, but was dissuaded from doing so just as we started. A nearer view—or rather, whiff—of the boat when they landed left me very glad indeed that I had not done so. In the north one becomes accustomed to a good many strong smells, and I had lived with the Eskimos a great deal, but that boat was the limit. Whale-oil and blubber had no terrors for me at that time, and I could go unwashed for a week, eat half-cooked, or wholly uncooked, food, and sleep on a 6-inch plank with any sailor, but I drew the line at that boat.

We spent one night at the encampment, though it was night only in name, for I was teaching the Eskimos in broad daylight at 2 a.m., and then we sailed away until we came to a large island on which we found some fifty large walrus which had been killed by the Eskimos that summer. On this island I caught a most beautiful eiderduck, which refused to leave the eggs, about twenty in number, upon which she was sitting. I, however, refused to disturb her or to take her eggs. The Eskimos and Indians of the north country are very fond of eggs in what may well be described as a " high " state; in fact, disgusting as it may seem to us, they really prefer having something to masticate in an egg. I must confess that I have made but one attempt to acquire this taste, and never wanted to try again.

On Sunday evening, the 31st of July, we came within sight of Marble Island. It lay about twenty miles to the north of us, and with the sun shining full upon it looked just like an immense iceberg, and might very easily have been taken for one. Another day's sail brought us to where the Eskimos were encamped on the mainland opposite the island, but before we could land a thick fog descended and blotted everything from view, and we were obliged to anchor. When the fog lifted next day we found ourselves hemmed in on every side by ice, though there had been no signs of it when we dropped the anchor. To sit in a small boat in the midst of large masses of ice charging down upon one with horrible grinding and crunching sounds is an experience likely to quicken the pulses of even the boldest. It is bad enough in a stout ship, as I have found in Hudson's Strait, but in a boat it is a thousand times worse.

A freshening gale compelled us to run some distance down Jones's Inlet as soon as we got clear of the ice. Several seas washed right over us, drenching everything: in addition to this it rained in torrents the whole time. Going down the Inlet for some miles we managed to run into a small bay, where we got a little shelter from the storm, but the rain continued so that for twenty-four hours we were unable to light a fire and could do nothing but try and sleep in wet blankets.

When at last the gale moderated we worked our way back to the Eskimo encampment. Fifty more of them came in the day we arrived, increasing the population of the temporary settlement to 150 souls. They were simply delighted to see me and earnestly begged me to stay with them permanently, but owing to the lateness of the season I could not venture to prolong my visit over two days. They were, indeed, very busy days spent in visiting the tents, having school for the children and holding services. Many of these people had never before heard the Gospel, though most of them had heard of the minister at Churchill. It was, indeed, most touching to see the way they listened whilst I tried to set before them the Fatherhood of God and the brotherhood of Christ. It made me wonder what the effect would be upon professing Christians if they could as grown-up men and women listen for the first time to the Gospel story. It would, I am sure, do away to a very large extent with the mere nominal Christianity of many of our churches.

On the voyage home, which was quite uneventful, we came across several other bands of Eskimos, but I could only stay with them a few hours whilst the men were trading. I consider that I came into contact with about five hundred of this interesting race during my month's voyage, so the time was not spent in vain.

To live, sleep, and eat in a 40-foot boat on the western shores of Hudson's Bay for four weeks is an undertaking I should hesitate to impose upon any man unless I wished him to have a taste of purgatory, but in the Lord's service physical misery is speedily forgotten in the consciousness that slowly but surely the inhabitants of the frozen north are being won for Christ. Even now the voice of prayer and praise is heard in many a snow-made *iglo*, and many times over on this trip did I hear the words, " *Koveasukpok ; Okperkpogook* "—" We rejoice; we believe."

CHAPTER XV

THE POLAR BEAR OF THE NORTH

THE polar bear of the north country is on the whole a very inoffensive animal, generally very shy of man. His food consists of seal-flesh, blubber, salmon, and other kinds of fish. On the rare occasions on which he has deliberately attacked man he has nearly always been driven to do so by the all-compelling force of hunger. But, on the other hand, if pursued and wounded he is no mean enemy, and then a man's life depends upon the reliability of his gun and on his marksmanship.

I saw a polar bear for the first time in the summer of 1884 when on my way along the coast from York Factory to Churchill. How we came upon him unawares as he lay asleep, and how he bolted panic-stricken when a gun was fired in the air, has already been related. A few years later, whilst I was stationed as missionary at Churchill, one of our Indians, a big strapping 6-footer, came across the traces of a polar bear whilst out hunting in the Cape Churchill district. Following the trail as only an Indian can, he at length observed the animal sitting on a low ridge. The bear, whose wariness easily foiled any further attempt at stalking, no sooner

114

perceived his enemy than he advanced to encounter him. The Indian fired, but unfortunately his gun missed fire (they use only shot-guns, not rifles), and the next moment he was struck to the ground by a blow from the bear's mighty paw. With the bear standing right over him the Indian's sole chance lay in feigning death. He lay perfectly still, scarcely daring to breathe, whilst the bear rolled him over several times; then the bear moved off a short distance, watching him as a cat watches a mouse. Seizing his opportunity the Indian was on his hands and knees in a moment, reaching for his gun, but too late, for with a bound of unexpected swiftness he was bowled over again, this time having his right shoulder very badly torn. Again he lay as dead, and the bear, after rolling him over several times, bruising him severely and watching for the slightest movement, went off and left him. The Indian, rendered cautious by his recent experience, allowed the animal to go unmolested, and then rose and walked to the Mission, nearly fifty miles away, where I dressed his injuries and heard his story, finding him much knocked about, badly bruised, and his shoulder terribly lacerated, though fortunately no bones were broken.

One summer the Rev. G. S. Winter, then missionary in charge at York Factory, paid us a visit at Churchill. He was unable to return, as he had come, by boat, but was obliged to walk along the coast. On his journey he camped one night with his companions, two Indians named James Begg and Harry Stag, at Stoney Creek, about fifty miles from York. A few willows or pieces of driftwood to form a wind-screen and a large fire of driftwood constitute a camp on the shores of the Bay in summer; tents are never carried, for, unlike missionaries in Africa or other parts of the world, the missionary in the far north cannot have a band of porters to carry his effects. After supper and prayers Mr. Winter and his companions rolled themselves in their blankets and were soon fast asleep. About two hours later, when it was quite dark and the fire had burned low, Harry Stag was awakened by the pressure of some heavy object on his leg. Peeping out from his blanket he was startled to perceive a polar bear standing right over him.

At the shout of "Bear in camp" all three were on the other side of the fire in the twinkling of an eye. The bear, surprised for the moment, quickly recovered his self-possession and prowled round the camp: then began an exciting though somewhat ludicrous chase around the fire. A firebrand failed to scare the visitor; in the confusion the campers had no time to seize any weapon; neither gun nor axe lay ready to hand, and, to make matters worse, Mr. Winter, who was very short-sighted, lost his glasses and could see nothing. The bear finally became tired of the game, and picking up a pair of "husky" boots made of sealskin and a pair of pants walked off a few paces to examine his prizes.

The Polar Bear of the North

This gave the breathless men an opportunity of securing a gun, but it was only loaded with small shot, and they could not find a bullet. Dissatisfied with the nature of his booty, the bear returned to the camp, and recommenced the novel pastime of chasing his quarry round and round the fire. Breaking away from the giddy whirl, the man with the gun made off out of the camp, and the bear after him. He fired, but the small shot did not stop the bear or damp his ardour, and the next instant the Indian came into sharp contact with mother earth with a great deal more violence than was agreeable. Evidently satisfied with this exhibition of his pugilistic prowess, the bear then returned to the camp and helped himself to a blanket, but the other man had by this time succeeded in loading his gun with ball, and bowled the bear right over with his first shot. He was not content, however, with this, and fired five more shots into the body of the bear. Then the other Indian rejoined the rest of the party and they sat around the camp fire until daylight enabled them to skin the animal. The bear's stomach was quite empty, a circumstance which explained his boldness in invading the camp as he did.

In the spring of 1893, when travelling from Churchill to York with dogs and sledge, we one day sighted a polar bear and two cubs as we were crossing a large plain nearly twenty miles wide. We managed to get between them and the sea, which was not far away. As soon as our dogs got wind of them they started in pursuit. After a chase of 10 miles we ran them into the woods where the snow was soft and deep. The mother bear could very easily have escaped from us but for her devotion to her offspring, which being only about the size of collie dogs became very tired and frequently lagged behind, when she would stop and whine for them to come up; when they got into the soft snow they could make no progress at all, and simply lay down. The mother bear would go on for some distance, then stop and call to them to come on, and when at last she saw they could not do this, and that we were getting close at hand, she came back and stood over her young ones to protect them; in this attitude we shot her, and knocked over the cubs with sticks. It seemed a rather cruel proceeding, but we had no animal food and very little of anything else, and we still had 100 miles to go before we could get any. The Indians also wanted the skin of the bear, for it meant money to them. Within twenty minutes of shooting the bear we were sitting round a camp fire eating bear steaks. My little daughter, then five years old, had one of the cubs as a doll for some time, and finally it was sent home to the Church Missionary Society, and is now, or was, in the Museum at Salisbury Square.

Polar-bear meat is very strong, in more senses than one. In the spring, after the bear has been hibernating for some months, it is not so bad, but in the fall, when the animals are fat, it is exceedingly fishy and fit only for the omnivorous Eskimo.

A friend of mine on a visit to us at Churchill was most anxious to taste polar-bear meat even though we were then in the month of October.

We managed to procure some from an Eskimo, and to humour him my wife cooked some of it, but she declined to bring it into the room, telling us that we must go into the kitchen if we wanted it. Accordingly we adjourned thither, and beheld on the table two plates each containing a small piece of meat simply swimming in oil. I had often eaten bear's flesh before, but always out in the open, and this particular specimen, being indoors, did not appeal to me. The odour of the thing defied description. My friend sniffed the morsel and turned up his nose, but manfully asserted that if I could eat it he could. In order to induce him to try I set him the example, though it was really hard work to do so; at last he managed to get a very small piece into his mouth, but immediately bolted for the kitchen door, coming back in a few moments minus the bear's meat and other things, and looking as he might have done on first being in a storm at sea. Two years later he wrote that he could still taste that bear's meat, and wanted no more.

CHAPTER XVI

TRAVELLING EXPERIENCES ON THE SHORES OF HUDSON'S BAY

THE year 1893 was a period of great change for us and also of very active work for me. Owing to the exceptional severity of the winter some of the Indians and Eskimos suffered greatly from privation and destitution. One whole party of Indians was very nearly starved to death, and one whole family of Eskimos actually perished from starvation.

In this year Archdeacon Winter and his family left York Factory, turning the Mission over to my care, no easy charge, as York and Churchill are nearly two hundred miles apart, with no road and no house between them.

In winter the journey had to be made on snowshoes, and in summer either by small open boat or on foot along the coast. In March I went to York by dog-sledge, and on this journey encountered the bear and cubs mentioned in the last chapter. During my stay, which lasted until after Easter, I had the pleasure of baptizing some Indian babies who had been carried over one hundred miles on their mother's back to be admitted into the outward fellowship of Christ's Church. On one occasion whilst I was there nearly fifty Indians knelt round the Lord's Table, many of whom had walked from one to two hundred miles in order to be present.

We made a special effort in returning home owing to the fineness of the weather, and accomplished the entire journey in four days, being an average of 50 miles a day—a very fair performance on snow-shoes—though I have known this beaten many a time by Indians. As a result, however, I was incapacitated for nearly a week, so that our haste was little to our advantage, only that I was home, and found all well after many weeks' absence.

In April the arrival of large parties of Eskimos, Chipewyans, and Crees, many of whom had suffered great hardships during the winter, gave me a lot of work to do in addition to the painting and finishing of the church, so that the time passed all too quickly.

In July we bade farewell to the Hudson's Bay officer, Mr. Spencer, who was leaving with his family for Winnipeg, after having been in the service of the Company at Churchill for twenty years. We parted with the greatest regret from those who had been such good friends to us, and especially so as Mrs. Spencer was the only white woman besides my wife within a radius of 200 miles; nay more, for there was no other white woman to the north of us.

The annual ship came in on the 13th of August, bringing us another year's supplies, for which we were deeply thankful. As a steamer had now

replaced the old sailing vessel, we were able to fore-
cast the arrival of our yearly supplies with much
more certainty than formerly.

On the 21st of the month, after the ship had left,
I started on another visit to York, going this time
by a schooner of 60 tons that had begun to run
between the two places. After a very pleasant
voyage of four days we reached York, and I spent
a very happy three weeks amongst the Indians at
the post, who had now been without a missionary
for a year. Services had, nevertheless, been regularly conducted on Sundays and weekdays alike by
one of their own number, an unpaid lay-worker.

My return journey was an experience never to be
forgotten. As the schooner was to be laid up at
York for the winter, three of us started back for
Churchill in a heavily laden York boat, about thirty
feet long, with no cabin or shelter of any kind.
We had been enjoying some delightful mid-Sep-
tember weather, but on the day we set sail a complete change took place: for two days we were detained at the mouth of the Hayes River, unable to
put out to sea, and without a tent or cabin in our
boat to shelter us from the continuous heavy rain.
A good run of 20 miles on the third day took us
across the mouth of the Nelson, but rain fell heavily
during the night, and in the morning we were
unable to leave until midday, as the tide was out.
When at last we did get under way the wind veered
to the north-east, so that, after running a short

distance, we were compelled to put in for the shore at high tide. Next day the tide never came near our boat, and it was impossible for the three of us to move her; so we had to stay where we were for six whole days of continuous hail, sleet, rain, and snow, with no tent or shelter of any kind, and with very little firewood and that only heavy driftwood, which would hardly burn at all. After six days of this misery we walked to the tent of an Indian, some eight miles away, sinking up to the knees in icy-cold water at every step. We spent the night there. It was not at all comfortable, but certainly better than lying in the rain. Next morning we returned to our boat and succeeded in getting her off, but, after having made only four miles' progress at the end of four hours' hard work, were again driven ashore by a heavy gale. Once more we were weatherbound, on this occasion for two days. Although we had been out from York ten days, we had only made some forty miles; our food supply was almost gone, and we were at least one hundred and fifty miles from home.

We had, however, no thought of turning back, for Churchill was home. The whole country was now covered with snow, and it seemed as if there were no chance of getting north with the boat, so we decided to abandon her and to continue our journey on foot. We started in a blinding snow-storm on the 25th of September, each man carrying his own kit and gun. The whole country was in a state of flood after the heavy rains, the swamps were lakes, the creeks rivers, and the rivers torrents. For six days we toiled on, sinking up to the knees through the ice, which had formed on the pools and swamps, and at night sleeping in our wet clothes wherever the darkness happened to come upon us. In crossing Owl River we were immersed up to the waist for two hours in the icy-cold water, lashed together with rope, and clinging to poles in order to prevent our being swept off our feet by the flood. At Broad River we were shoulder-high in water for over an hour before we could get across, and a heavy storm of rain, hail, and snow overtook us as we were crossing Cape Churchill, one of the most desolate, dreary places in the whole world. For hours we wandered about in the " Eastern Creeks," and at last reached " Knight's Hill Beacon " so exhausted that we lay on the open ground all night in spite of the downpour of rain.

Captain Hawes, one of my companions, was in a very bad state, and I feared that he would succumb.

Next day we started more cheerfully as it was a fine day, though we had nothing for breakfast but tea; we lost our way, however, and, after wandering for four hours, returned to our starting-point. Again we set out, and found a trail leading to Churchill. Though we were now only 25 miles from home, our weakness and exhaustion was such that we failed to reach the place and spent the night instead in abject misery, with no food other than the berries that we could find along the route, and no ammunition. We had been exposed to rain, hail, sleet or snow every day since leaving the boat; as a rule we were walking through deep water most of the time, and at night had to endure five or six degrees of frost, wet to the skin, and without covering of any kind, except our one blanket each. I have never experienced a more trying journey in all my twenty years in the Bay.

The people at Churchill had almost given us up for lost, as the whole countryside there was covered with full a foot of snow. In order to cross the Churchill River we had to commandeer a small, leaky skiff, which we very fortunately found on the shore, and had a very hard time in getting it across without going to the bottom; had we not crossed on that day, we should have been compelled to wait until the two miles of water froze fast, nearly a month later, and as there was neither food nor shelter on the south side, nor a chance of shooting anything, since we had guns but no ammunition, we should inevitably have been frozen to death. So completely exhausted was I that I had to spend a full week in bed in order to recuperate.

The wintry weather continued, though it was only the 1st of October. The snow had come to stay, and though the river did not set fast till a month later, the quantity of heavy floating ice made it impassable.

About the middle of October we were greatly

astonished by the arrival of two white men from the north, members of J. B. Tyrrell's party, which was frozen in some thirty miles to the north of Churchill. They had been exploring the Barren Lands, and had come out on Hudson's Bay at Chesterfield Inlet. Coming down the coast from there, they had met even worse weather than that which had overtaken us on the way from York. Compelled at last to abandon the greater part of their outfit and to push on with all possible speed to Churchill, they had become frozen in just north of Seal River, many of them being scarcely able to walk or stand. As their food supply was almost gone, and they were a party of nine, two men were sent out to see if they could find the post, but returned next day without having seen any trace of it. A second party was then sent out, and most fortunately for them happened to come across some hunters from the post, who brought them in.

A relief party was at once organized, food sent out to them, and in two days the whole party of eight were brought into the post by the dog-teams, and only just in time, for a few more days of privation and exposure would have caused a fatal ending to the sufferings of some of the party. J. B. Tyrrell and his brother, J. W. Tyrrell, were both very ill, and two of the men were badly frozen, one of them being obliged to have the toes of one foot amputated. After nearly a month's stay at Churchill the whole party, with the exception of one man, who was compelled to remain at York until the summer, as he was unable to walk, was sent on by dog-teams to York, and thence by way of Oxford House to Winnipeg, where they arrived in safety.

This year was one of strange adventures and incidents. In addition to the events narrated above, our new church narrowly escaped destruction by fire in November, and our little mission house twice caught fire owing to a defective chimney. Fire in the north is a most terrible thing, as it is impossible to obtain water for six months in the year, except by melting ice and snow. There is no hope of saving a building once the flames begin to spread. We have much to thank God for in that in all our twenty years' residence there we were never afflicted by a fire of a serious nature; but the most unwearied vigilance is necessary, and the ever-present possibility of an outbreak is a source of constant anxiety.

CHAPTER XVII

KAYAKING

AN Eskimo *kayak*, or canoe, is a craft of most ingenious construction and much lighter even than the Indian birchbark. It is as a rule from sixteen to twenty feet long, but built to take one man only. The *kayaks* in use on the western shores of the Bay are only from twenty to twenty-four inches wide, and rounded on the bottom. On the east coast they are wider as a rule, and made with a flat bottom. The framework of the *kayak* is composed of hundreds of small pieces of wood beautifully fitted together and sewn with seal-line, not a nail or peg entering into its construction. It is covered with sealskin put on wet, and most wonderfully sewn together. An ordinary man can lift it with one hand and place it on his head.

The single occupant uses a double-bladed paddle. This is not only a means of propulsion, but serves also as a balancing pole for this most frail and ticklish craft. The slightest thing will overturn a *kayak*, and when overturned in the water it is by no means an easy thing to extricate oneself. I once had a very narrow escape when I hung for some seconds by the legs before succeeding in freeing myself and swimming ashore.

ESKIMOS IN KAYAK

Kayaking

The Eskimos, however, are wonderful watermen and very rarely have an upset, though they often venture far out to sea, even out of sight of land sometimes, and shoot or spear fish, seals, and even whales from their *kayaks*. A white man's first experience is invariably an unpleasant one, for he is almost sure to go over, and no Indian will use a *kayak* on any account.

A large party of Eskimos had been staying at the old fort for two months, and when they started for the north in the middle of July, 1894, I decided to go with them in order to visit their tribesmen as far north as Marble Island. The party con-sisted of nearly one hundred Chipewyans as well as the Eskimos. These were all packed into two large coast-boats, whilst a third contained our party with a crew of two Eskimos, two Chipewyans, one Cree, and an English-speaking native of Churchill. When we dropped down the river to join the others at the old fort, we found the Indians and Eskimos busy embarking men, women, children, dogs, tents, goods and chattels without semblance of order into two boats, where they were left to stow them-selves and their belongings as best they could when they got out to sea. A fair wind betokened a pleasant voyage, but (there are many " buts " in travelling on Hudson's Bay) about six miles out from the mouth of the river we found ourselves confronted by a wall of ice, and were compelled to return to " Sea Horse Gully," where many of the Indians

I

decided to walk rather than trust themselves at sea amongst so much ice.

As canoe-men on rivers and lakes the Indians are not to be beaten, but they are no sailors and greatly fear the sea, whereas the Eskimos are in their element there. A second attempt brought us to Long Point, about forty miles from the post; here the ice, which was packed close inshore, rendered further progress to the north impossible. The whole party of over two hundred persons then landed and encamped. A heavy gale delayed us here for three days, causing us the loss of one of the boats owing to the ice-pressure; but at last we managed to get away, and made 20 miles more until a solid mass of ice, reaching as far as one could see to the north, impeded our journey, and detained us for another week. The coast to the north was packed with ice as if in mid-winter. Our slow rate of progress, some sixty miles in twelve days, and the forbidding aspect of the ice, were circumstances which induced me to give up all hope of being able to reach Marble Island and return in time to meet the annual ship which was due to arrive about the middle of August. On the 28th of July, therefore, I made up my mind to return, and, after some trouble, succeeded in inducing two of the Eskimos to take me back on their *kayaks* to Long Point, where I hoped to catch one of our boats which had been left there before it returned to Churchill.

The two *kayaks* were accordingly lashed together,

so as to form a small raft about eighteen feet long and three feet wide. Stowing ourselves and our camp outfit upon this, we hoisted a blanket for a sail in order to take advantage of the fair wind which was blowing, and put out to sea.

I found the situation somewhat alarming at first, seated as I was within a few inches of the water, which was bitterly cold and constantly washed over us. After threading our way amongst large ice-floes for about two hours the wind fell, and we came to a standstill, as it was impossible to use the paddles to any good effect with the *kayaks* lashed together.

The Eskimos said we must reconstruct our raft so as to enable each man to use his paddle; we therefore landed on an ice-floe, and, parting the *kayaks*, lashed them together with poles, about four feet apart, so that each man could use his double-bladed paddle. The kettles, blankets, food, etc., were placed on the back of one *kayak*, and I took my seat on the back of the other, sitting bolt upright with no support for my back and only a small line alongside to assist me in keeping my balance. Every dip of the paddles immersed my legs in the icy-cold water. In such a situation a calculation of one's swimming powers affords but slight consolation. Several hours' travelling in this manner failed to bring us to Long Point, owing to the thickly packed fields of ice, so we landed for the night in a dreary and desolate place, where we were fortunate enough to find a few pieces of driftwood to make a fire—a very welcome discovery, as it rained all night, and we had no shelter but our blankets.

In the morning the ice had opened out a little, and an early start enabled us to reach Long Point about three o'clock in the afternoon, travelling as before. I was so badly cramped and so stiff with cold that I could not walk or even stand, but had to roll off the *kayaks* and lay rubbing my legs until they got some power back again. To my extreme disappointment I found that the boat had left the previous morning.

A stay of two days in an Eskimo tent gave me an excellent opportunity of teaching the natives, but the circumstances were somewhat trying. One must have a stomach of iron to eat in the company of a crowd of women and children, all devouring raw salmon or seal's meat and drinking whale-oil, the very smell of which is sufficient to cause sea-sickness. To complete the picture, imagine the presence, in one corner, of a woman going over the head of her child with her fingers in simian fashion, and devouring the results of her explorations.

Since the boat had gone, my only chance of catching her was to push on to Seal River, a distance of 15 miles on the *kayaks*, and I had some difficulty in getting two of the men to go with me, for they were anxious to get north.

However, I succeeded at last, and we started as the day was fine. In spite of the rough sea, which drenched me continually, we hoped to reach our destination in one day, but, as luck would have it, failed to do so, and spent a night of the usual discomfort on a small rock, without a fire, and with nothing to eat but raw meat. We had hoped to catch the boat at Seal River, but when we reached the encampment were met with the words, "*Oomeak nouk*"—"No boat." My last hope was now gone, and I knew not what to do: the Eskimos were most anxious to return, and I could not walk home from there, as there was a large and deep river to cross. Finally I got two of them to promise to put me across this river, from which point I had to walk home, a distance of 20 miles. I started on my solitary tramp at 4 a.m., carrying all my outfit, fully forty pounds in weight, along a route which took me through swamps, and without a vestige of a trail. The day was hot, and I was nearly devoured by black flies and mosquitoes. In the afternoon a heavy thunderstorm came on, but fortunately no rain for a time. I lost my way and wandered for some hours on the rocks behind Churchill until night came on, and with it a heavy rain, which soon drenched me to the skin and seemed to make my pack a ton weight. By the aid of the lightning flashes, I picked my way over the rocks, and at 10 p.m., after eighteen hours' walking, I stumbled into the little mission house, greatly to the astonishment of my family, who were under the impression that I was some four or five hundred miles away at Marble Island.

A Thousand Miles from a Post Office

When the annual ship came in that summer we parted from our only child, whom we were sending to England in the care of our English servant. Though they left us in August, it was not until the end of the following February that we got news of their safe arrival in England. How much we missed her can be understood only by people situated as we were, with no friends or companions near, except Indians and Eskimos. The departure of one of many children is a distinct loss; the parting from an only child, as in our case, constituted one of the greatest trials of our missionary life, but for her sake it was a wise and necessary thing.

CHAPTER XVIII

VISITORS AT CHURCHILL

THE winter of 1893–94 passed pleasantly enough, with the usual spells of very severe weather, which made it impossible to go out except clad very much like a " Husky " (our usual term for Eskimo), and very difficult to keep warm even indoors. Towards the end of February I left home in very bad weather to visit my outlying district of York Factory with my team of dogs and Indian boy Sammy. We were snowbound for two days at Minister's Lobstick, a most dreary place, so called from a rather high tree, from which many years before Archdeacon Kirkby cut the lower branches in order to form a landmark. This was a sort of " footing " expected from new-comers, and in the olden days, when liquor was freely carried and given out at the Bay posts, an opportunity for the men to secure a " drink all round." Now that liquor has been shut out for many years, this sort of thing is very rarely done.

Our camp being on very open ground, we suffered greatly from the cold, as we could get but very little firewood, and one morning we woke up, like the Irishman, to find ourselves buried, but it was in snow, more than a foot deep. We reached York on the eighth day, instead of on the sixth, as we should have done.

For six weeks I remained at York teaching and holding services, at which I met quite a large number of Cree Indians, one of whom had tramped in the most severe weather 100 miles in order to have his child baptized, and many others, both men and women, had walked from one to two hundred miles in order to take advantage of the opportunity to kneel around the Lord's Table.

The early spring of that year made our return journey extremely trying. We started to return on Easter Monday, by which time nearly all the snow had disappeared, and, though the ice underneath was still firm, the creeks and swamps were full of water and many of the lakes covered with about six inches of water. Up to our knees in this we waded the 4 miles of swamp between the Fort and the Nelson River, and at the point where we crossed, 7 miles wide, there was nearly a foot of water on the ice, rendering the task of getting a loaded sledge and dogs across an undertaking of the greatest difficulty. The absence of snow and the sodden condition of the ground made travelling extremely hard work, and no dry spots were to be found for camping places. Pressing on, nevertheless, in spite of these discomforts and trials, on the sixth day we entered the eastern woods, 25 miles from Churchill. The weather, which up to that time had been remarkably mild, then underwent a sudden change; a north-west wind caused the thermometer to drop a long way below zero that night, and the rain and thaw ceased.

The route from the eastern woods to Churchill lay through swamps and small lakes, which we found in the morning coated with about an inch of ice. Though this would easily bear the weight of a man, as soon as our sledges got on to it they broke through into the foot or so of water below. There was, of course, no danger of going through the under ice, for that was firm enough, but we had to pull, tug, and lift our sledge and dogs to the other side, and it was not quite like working in the South Seas. Our clothes, wet to the middle, froze upon us as soon as we got out of the water, and it was rather like running in a sack; our snow-shoes fell to pieces owing to the wet and the rough passage. At 9 p.m., some ten hours after we started, we arrived home, footsore and weary beyond measure, and coated with ice to the middle. Several of my toes were very badly frozen, and I lost the whole set of toe-nails. My snow-shoes, the only ones that had remained intact, weighed eight pounds each when I took them off, and my trousers were so stiff in their icy coat that they easily stood upright. For several weeks after I suffered severely from the effects of this trip; but I was able to resume my duties before long, and to put away remembrance of these hardships, as I had so often done in the north.

The arrival of a large number of Eskimos and Chipewyans in the spring and summer kept me very busy until the annual ship reached us in the first week of August. Now that the Company had put on a steamer we had no longer to endure the weeks of anxious watching for the belated appearance of a sailing vessel. This steamer, the *Eric*, performed her voyage for seven years without having been detained in the Strait for an hour; in the Bay, however, once or twice she ran into heavy field ice off the western coast, on one occasion having had to plough her way through fully sixty miles of it. Captain Gray, an old experienced whaler, had been accustomed nearly all his life to ice navigation, which makes all the difference in the world, for no man can sail the northern seas and navigate ice simply because he has navigated the Atlantic or southern seas. It takes him years to learn the different tricks of the ice floes and bergs.

After the departure of the ship we were left to the pleasant monotony of our daily lives, and given time to prepare for the coming winter.

On the 1st of October we were again surprised by the unexpected arrival of Mr. J. B. Tyrrell, of the Geological Survey. We heard nothing of his going into the north country again. He was accompanied by Mr. Munro Ferguson, A.D.C. to the then Governor-General, Lord Aberdeen. Their expedition had crossed the Barren Lands, along the course of the Kazan River, and had emerged on Hudson's Bay at Eskimo Point, some two hundred and fifty miles north of Churchill.

Visitors at Churchill

Overtaken by very bad weather, though not so bad as the year before, they had managed to push on to the Mission before becoming frozen in, and escaped with a few minor casualties. Further travelling by canoe along the shores of the Bay was out of the question, and they were compelled to wait until the freezing of the lakes and rivers permitted them to make their way across country by dog sledge to Split Lake on the Nelson River, thence to Norway House, and from there to Winnipeg, where they arrived in safety. This was the first time that this route had ever been used, but since then the Mounted Police and others have crossed that way, and they have now a well-defined trail. It was a very different thing in 1894, when Mr. Tyrrell first attempted it.

As the Hudson's Bay Company's premises lacked suitable accommodation Mr. Tyrrell and Mr. Ferguson lived with us for eight weeks in our little mission house, though as we had but one spare bed they had, as we say in the north, to " double up," but I do not think they minded this very much, as it was at least better than being in camp on the shores of the Bay.

Their warm interest in our work and people and their presence in the house made the visit a real pleasure to us; visitors were so rare and infrequent in those days. On the other hand, too many visitors might have a rather devastating effect on one's winter stock of provisions, which could on no account be replenished until the following summer. A shortage of various necessities did occur occasionally, with somewhat amusing results. I remember well that one year we almost ran out of matches, but being well supplied with candles we hit upon the economical expedient of burning candles to save matches.

An amusing account of his stay at the mission house was written by Mr. Ferguson on his return to civilization, in which the necessary " Jack-of-all trades " ability of the missionary to Hudson's Bay is well illustrated. This narrative was published in the *Montreal Diocesan College Magazine* for March and April, 1895.

CHAPTER XIX

THE BISHOPS OF THE NORTH

THE whole of the Hudson's Bay district lay within the Diocese of Moosonee until the year 1902. In that year the Diocese of Keewatin was founded, as the enormous stretch of territory under the jurisdiction of the Bishop of Moosonee rendered effective supervision of the diocese an extremely difficult, if not impossible, task. The Bishop resided at Moose Factory, in the extreme south of James's Bay, from which point a diocesan visit to the York and Churchill stations, to say nothing of other stations hundreds of miles away in the interior, meant a journey of some thousands of miles, on snow-shoes or by open boat, across trackless country.

No system of communication existed between the various posts on the Bay itself, except in the south. It will be remembered that when travelling from Moose Factory to York, shortly after my arrival in the country, I had been obliged to make a detour of thousands of miles as far south as Lake Superior in order to cover a journey of some six or eight hundred miles.

Bishop Horden, the first Bishop of Moosonee, visited Churchill in 1881, the year before I came out, and spent some months at the post. In 1887 he revisited the station, but in that year we had been compelled to go to England on account of my wife's unsatisfactory state of health, and consequently we could not have the pleasure of receiving him or getting any help from his visit.

In the eight years from 1887 to 1895 our mission post remained unvisited by a Bishop. Bishop Horden died at Moose Factory early in 1892, after forty-one years of most self-sacrificing and successful work amongst the Indians of the north.

He was succeeded by Bishop Newnham, the present Bishop of Saskatchewan (now resigned and living in England), whose interest in the northern stations of the diocese made him most anxious to undertake an early journey to the north country. With this intention he left Moose towards the end of September, 1894, but after ascending the Moose River as far as Missinābie he decided to postpone his visit until the following spring or, rather, early summer. A thousand-mile journey on snow-shoes in the depth of winter is not an undertaking to be lightly entered upon. Having altered his plans he spent the winter and spring in Eastern Canada, and then went west to Winnipeg in time to catch the first boat across that lake. Early in June he set forth along the well-known route in the north—*i.e.*, across Lake Winnipeg—by boat to within some twenty miles of Norway House, then down the rivers and lakes by canoe to the coast at York Factory, and from York to Churchill on board a small York boat.

On the 14th of July he reached his most northerly point, greatly to our relief, for we had been anxiously expecting his arrival for some time. I had not seen my Bishop for thirteen years, consequently Bishop Newnham's visit realized a long-cherished wish, and raised hopes of further progress and expansion in the near future.

These hopes were by no means doomed to disappointment, for we were delighted to find that the Bishop had with him an assistant in the person of Mr. F. Buckland, who was to organize a Mission still farther north than Churchill. It had always been a matter of keen regret to me that we were unable to reach these northern people.

The Bishop spent a very busy ten days with us. Some of the English-speaking natives were confirmed, and four Eskimos, whom we had prepared, were baptized, the first of these people on the western shores to be admitted into the outward Church. As a considerable number of both Eskimos and Indians happened to be staying at the place, the Bishop had a very good opportunity of observing the work of the Mission and also of studying its needs. He congratulated us upon the splendid appearance of our little mission house and church, both of which we had built with our own hands, and was especially pleased by the earnest attention and reverence shown by both Indians and Eskimos.

Work amongst the latter is exceedingly difficult owing to their nomadic habits. They have no settled villages, and only come into the post at long intervals.

At the Bishop's request I accompanied him on his return journey to York Factory, where we arrived after an uneventful trip along the coast. Deer and ducks were very numerous, and mosquitoes even more so. The Bishop, in discussing these annoying pests, said he had never before endured such persecution as we had suffered on that trip, although during his thirty years' residence in Canada he had spent several summers at Moose Factory, where they are reputed to be especially bad. It seems that the farther north one goes the worse these little pests become; the shorter the summer season the more actively they live their brief life.

At York quite a number of the Indians were confirmed, and the Rev. William Dick of Trout Lake, a full-blooded Indian, was admitted to the priesthood. He had been ordained deacon by Bishop Horden some years previously.

When, at the end of five days, we left for our respective homes, I had the good luck to secure a passage in a small 60-ton schooner, a much more comfortable mode of travelling than in a small boat with no accommodation or a tramp on foot along the bleak, swampy coast. Bishop Newnham had, however, a much more trying trip. From Severn, 275 miles down the coast in a small canoe is no easy journey, and after that he had to make his way across country to Albany, on one occasion coming very near to losing his life in a swamp. Indeed, but for his Indians, he would have done so. The last stage of the journey from Albany to Moose Factory was quite easy, and he arrived safe home just about the end of October. Thus, in order to visit three of his Missions, the Bishop had been absent from his home just thirteen months, during which time he had travelled 4,000 miles, fully half the distance by canoe or small open boat. The unworkable extent of the diocese, and the necessity for a new northern bishopric, needs no further illustration.

When we arrived at Churchill, after a tedious voyage of ten days, during which we were often fogbound, we were greatly surprised to find the Hudson's Bay Company's whaling vessel *Persever-ance*, commanded by Captain Murray, in the harbour. Having spent the previous winter in Repulse Bay, and the summer whaling in the northern seas, she was now awaiting the arrival of our annual ship the *Eric*, in order to take on supplies for another year's cruise. During their sojourn in the northern seas, Captain and Mrs. Murray had a son born to them, who, I believe, was the first white baby born within the arctic circle, and I had the pleasure of baptizing this child.

On the 21st of August the *Eric* arrived after a most ill-fated voyage. The first mate died on the sixth day out from Peterhead, and in Hudson's Strait the ship was detained by dense fog for three whole weeks, during which she very narrowly escaped being wrecked on Mansfield Island.

Mrs. Murray went home on the *Eric,* and when the *Perseverance* had taken on her supplies she started again for the north, taking Mr. Buckland with her as a passenger. He had willingly agreed with my suggestion of a winter's work amongst the Eskimos. I set before him very clearly and frankly the hardships of the life he would have to lead, but he expressed himself as quite willing to face them, and so, Captain Murray having kindly consented to take him, he departed on the 26th of August.

Thus again we were left to face the old humdrum life at Churchill. The visit of the Bishop, my journey to York, and the unexpected arrival of the *Per-severance,* had given us an unwonted amount of excitement that summer.

It almost seemed to us as if the rush and commotion of the busy outside world were at last reaching us at Churchill, " the last house in the world."

FIG. 33.   NUELTIN LAKE TRADING POST AND MISSION

CHAPTER XX

A THOUSAND MILES ON SNOW-SHOES

In the early days, and even up to 1882, York Factory was the port of entry for all the western country—at least, in so far as the Hudson's Bay Company was concerned.

As nearly all the supplies for the trading posts passed through it, the Company maintained a large staff of workmen and clerks at this important distributing centre, and also gave employment to most of the able-bodied Indians of the district during the summer when there was no hunting.

The decline of this post, as one may readily conjecture, dates from the completion of the Canadian Pacific Railway. Work could no longer be found for the four or five hundred Indians who spent the summer at the post, and they began gradually to drift away into the interior. Many of them pitched their tents on the Nelson River at a place called Split Lake, some three hundred miles away.

The excellency of the hunting and fishing there attracted a large number of the Indians, most of them from York and a few from Norway House and Cross Lake, until there was a settlement of nearly two hundred of them on the shores of Split

Lake. Their rapidly increasing numbers led the Company to establish a trading post amongst them.

These Indians were all Christians, most of them having been baptized at York Factory, but the inaccessibility of this latest settlement in the interior placed them beyond the reach of the missionary, and their spiritual welfare was left entirely in their own hands. Divine worship was maintained as well as possible, some of them always conducting services on Sundays, but they naturally felt that they were being neglected and going backward, and begged repeatedly that a minister might visit them or that a teacher might be sent to their assistance.

It was an exceedingly difficult matter to reach Split Lake from York in winter, and in summer almost impossible at that time, as no one had ever travelled much in that part. Furthermore, at that time, 1896, we had no missionary at York, that post remaining without one from the departure of the Rev. G. S. Winter in 1892 until 1898. As already related, York, 200 miles away from Churchill, was left in my care, and two or three visits were all I could manage in the course of a year. It was impossible to include Split Lake in my ministrations.

Bishop Newnham, in his visitation of 1895, was most anxious to include Split Lake in his itinerary, but found it utterly impossible, and requested me to visit it and report to him on the prospects of establishing a Mission in that district, as the Indians greatly desired it. This meant a tramp of between three and four hundred miles on snow-shoes through an almost unknown country. However, I communicated with our Indian catechist at York, Joseph Kitchekesik (Heavenly Man), and arranged to meet him on the arrival of the winter packet at Churchill in January. In spite of his unfamiliarity with the country we were to traverse, I felt confident of his native ability as a guide to find his way.

With a team of five " husky " dogs and an Indian half-breed boy as driver, we started about the middle of February, taking with us twelve days' provisions, ample as we thought for the journey we contemplated, and quite as much as we could carry, for we reckoned on obtaining fresh supplies from the deer, rabbits, and ptarmigan we expected to meet with on the way. We relied also on being able to procure additional supplies at Split Lake.

A rather prolonged spell of ill-health in the autumn and early winter made me somewhat indisposed to undertake such a journey, but, on the other hand, there was no one else to go, and I did not like to back out of a promise given to my Bishop.

From the Churchill River some miles from the post we emerged, via the Deer River, on to a large treeless plain, where we met with a very severe blizzard. Impelled by necessity we kept on, and at length reached the shelter of some woods. Here we were detained for a day, and for several days afterwards pressed on through blizzards so blinding that we could not see twenty yards in front of us. The difficulties of travelling with the thermometer between thirty-five and forty below zero, and the wind blowing in our faces at fully forty miles an hour, may be more easily imagined than described. A heavy fall of snow taxed the powers and endurance of our dogs to the utmost, although both Joseph and I went ahead in order to make a trail for them. The dogs' food alone weighed nearly two hundred and fifty pounds.

With the hope of coming across some Indians, of whom we had heard, we struck across country in a south-easterly direction, but becoming confused by the incessant gales we bore away too far to the east and missed a chain of lakes we knew to exist in that part of the country, but reached the Indian encampment on our sixth day out, only to find its deserted appearance explained by a birchbark note informing us that, owing to the scarcity of game, the Indians had left the neighbourhood. Game of every kind seemed to have deserted the country, and we were unable to shoot anything.

On leaving the Indian encampment, we entered a thickly wooded country where the depth and heaviness of the snow greatly impeded the dogs in spite of the fact that two of us were always ahead to break the trail. Travelling in this manner day after day, well aware that we were lost, and that our provisions were dwindling with unpleasant rapidity, we pressed steadily on in the direction of the Nelson

River, which would at least lead us down to the coast at York Factory. We had now been out twelve days, and when we camped that night things did not look too bright. Next afternoon, however, we came quite unexpectedly upon an old Indian trail running south, almost obliterated and invisible to any but Indian eyes; this, our guide was confident, would take us to the lakes we had missed, where we might find Indians from whom we could obtain fish both for ourselves and dogs.

We gave the dogs their last meal that night, and early next morning resumed our journey in a much more hopeful frame of mind. After some hours of heavy tramping we came out upon the first of the lakes and were able to form an idea of how far we had wandered from our true course.

No difficulty was experienced in finding the Indian shacks, but to our extreme disappointment not only were they deserted but their condition and the presence of the carcases of several dogs gave ample evidence of destitution and starvation.

On the evening of the same day we succeeded in overtaking the Indians, whom we found encamped in the woods when we came upon them. They were entirely without food—fish, rabbits and ptarmigan having disappeared from the district; they were trying to make their way to the trading post, distant two or three days' journey, in order to obtain relief. Two or three of them, in the last stages of exhaustion, were unable to walk or even to stand. A boy of sixteen, belonging to one of two families who had come from York, became lost in a gale, and though they spent several days in looking for him he was never found, and evidently died from exposure.

It was a most heart-rending sight to see these poor creatures camping thus in the woods; and our inability to render them immediate assistance only served to increase the pity of it. Reduced as we were to one scanty meal a day, with no food at all for the dogs, we could only give them a little tea and sugar, and promises of help when we reached the trading post. To share our last morsels with them would have meant slow starvation for all of us.

When we finally reached Split Lake on the third day after we left the Indians, our dogs had been for three days without food, and we ourselves had to be content with a drink of tea in the morning followed by a very scanty meal at the end of the day's tramp. We had been eighteen days on our trip from Churchill, and the combined effects of exposure and lack of sufficient food had tested our powers of endurance to the utmost. Our half-starved dogs were almost in a state of collapse and scarcely able to drag themselves along. Assistance was immediately dispatched to the starving Indians, and a few days later, in the last stages of exhaustion, they were all brought in to the post.

Split Lake in those days consisted of three small log-cabins, one of which, boasting one room only, was the home of the officer in charge. This room,

REV. J. LOFTHOUSE HAULING SLEDGE

ESKIMO DOGS AND SLEDGE

about twenty feet long by eighteen wide, was furnished with a simplicity to which the traditional Spartan would, I think, have strongly objected.

The furniture consisted of a box-stove in the centre of the room, a bed in each of two corners, and a rough couch against one wall. All of course were home-made and of the roughest kind, and there were no chairs of any sort.

I was most heartily welcomed by the man in charge, a Red River half-breed, and, after some conversation, acceded with alacrity to his suggestion of a wash, as I had had no opportunity of washing or of changing my clothes for nearly three weeks. But when I perceived what facilities the shanty possessed, a feeling of amusement almost overcame my chagrin and disappointment.

In obedience to his father's orders, the son of the house, a boy of twelve, placed a stool at my disposal, a tin dish containing not more than a pint of water, and a towel no larger than a pocket-handkerchief, and by no means white or clean, and indicated that the preparations were complete. However, in spite of the limited means at my disposal, and the presence of several Indian women, I managed fairly well, and at least got off the upper coating, and then sat down to a most welcome meal of sturgeon, a royal fish which is unknown to us at Churchill.

I remained at Split Lake for ten days, hospitably

entertained by the officer in charge, and sharing the daily life and single room of the family.

To the 150 Indians at that time dwelling at the post or in the vicinity my coming was a source of the greatest satisfaction and delight. Our services, held three or four times a day, were thronged with worshippers. I remember on one occasion journeying 50 miles in one day in order to administer Holy Communion to an old Indian woman, a devout Christian, whom I had known as a resident of York Factory for many years.

Another event which stands out prominently in my memory was a meeting attended by the chief and councillors, at which they gladly undertook to construct a school-house if we would only send them a teacher. I promised to send my guide, Joseph Kitchekesik, the next summer, and later on to appoint an ordained man. Of the seventy-five families which made up the population of the native village, many had dwelt in that neighbourhood for years without anyone to look after their spiritual welfare; yet I found that services were being conducted regularly by the chief, and that the Lord's Day was observed much more strictly than in any civilized town or village I know.

Our dogs seemed to have recovered completely when we left Split Lake to return home via York Factory, 300 miles distant, but three days later two of them died, and we had to help the survivors in hauling the load. Owing to the heaviness of the trail, our rate of progress was very slow, so that we did not reach the coast at York until the eleventh day, both tired out and without food.

Letters reached me on the 11th of April, just two months after I had left home, from which I learned that my wife was far from well and feeling much anxiety on my account. In order to reassure her as soon as possible, therefore, I left York on the 13th, accompanied by my boy-driver, and three dogs, for Churchill, where we arrived after a very tiresome journey of seven days through soft snow. My wife was very greatly relieved by my arrival.

During the ten weeks of my absence she had never heard a word of, or from, me, and whilst I was tramping a thousand miles on my snow-shoes, she had been left alone except for the companionship of an Indian girl. Battling with storms and starvation is far less trying than such waiting and watching. No one living in civilized or even in semi-civilized lands can at all realize what loneliness means in the north—the silence, the vast solitudes, and the awful feeling of helplessness they engender. These can only be realized by those who have endured them.

CHAPTER XXI

ACROSS THE NORTHERN BARREN LANDS

THERE was quite a large number of both Chipewyans and Eskimos who seldom if ever came to Churchill. These people lived chiefly to the north-west of the post, away on the barren lands. For a long time I had wished to visit them and see if anything could be done for them, but up to 1896 I had never been able to get away. The work of the Mission was now, however, on a more settled basis, and, early in July, 1896, I was able to leave Churchill in my small Peterborough canoe, with two Indians, taking with us a month's supply of food, for we were not at all sure of meeting any Indians or Eskimos, the country being so vast that one can easily travel in it for a month and not meet a soul.

It was our intention to explore the Tha-anni and Fish Rivers, which enter Hudson's Bay about one hundred miles north of Churchill; they had never been ascended by a white man, as far as I could gather, and their courses were but vaguely known from native descriptions.

We started auspiciously on a beautifully fine day. The ice had cleared off early from the coast, so that we were able to paddle across Button's Bay in four

156

hours, a journey which once took me, following the indentations of the coast, eighteen hours to accomplish. We were greatly pleased at reaching North River in such quick time, and still more so when a fresh breeze sprang up by the aid of which we sailed past Seal River, one of the most dangerous spots on the coast, almost to Long Point, 40 miles in a direct line from Churchill. At Long Point, which we reached at 8 a.m. next morning, we found one Eskimo family, with whom we spent a short time, and then pressed on. Shortly after, resuming our journey, a strong head-wind compelled us to put ashore and camp at a spot where the ubiquitous mosquito seemed to be particularly bloodthirsty.

On the following day, after passing Egg Island, we turned down a deep inlet into which the Tha-anni and Fish Rivers flow. This proved to be a most difficult place for canoeing; the ebb-tide recedes at least ten miles from the shore, which is very low and flat, and in the shallow water big stones were visible on every hand, and many more just within a few inches of the surface. In this dangerous situation we had the misfortune to be overtaken by a most severe thunderstorm. We could neither land nor seek any shelter on the water: for a time we were in the gravest danger, and I made sure we would be dashed to pieces.

With the passing of the rain I beheld a sight which in its enthralling beauty made me for a time at least oblivious of the precarious situation in which we were placed. The sky seawards was entirely obscured by a mass of dense black clouds, and, against this dark background, from north to south, appeared a series of seven distinct rainbows in concentric arcs. The brilliancy of their marvellous colouring stood out with startling vividness and furnished an awe-inspiring spectacle such as has been vouchsafed to few men. It was a sight of wondrous splendour, destined to live in the memory for ever. One becomes accustomed to most wonderful natural sights in the north country, and I have seen many, but never anything equal to this.

We managed at last to make the shore at a point where there was neither firewood nor fresh water, but we dared not put out to sea again in the rough water which followed in the wake of the storm, and had to stay there; after going about three miles through swamps we managed to get some rather brackish water and a few sticks of driftwood, so that we were able to get a cup of tea, the traveller's one comfort in the north.

Next day the sea had gone down somewhat, and, after a very hard day's paddling, we reached the mouth of the Tha-anni and landed on an island completely covered with the nests of eiderducks. In half an hour we gathered over three hundred eggs. Many of them were more suitable for electioneering purposes than for the breakfast table, but this blemish rather enhanced their value in the eyes of my Indians.

Across the Northern Barren Lands

In spite of the large volume of water which comes down these rivers, a small boat would find great difficulty in finding a channel of sufficient depth owing to the extreme breadth of their mouths and the consequent shallowness of the water. Some miles higher up the river the banks rise to a height of 20 feet. The country on both sides is one vast mossy plain, without the vestige of a tree or shrub upon it.

We spent the next day, Sunday, in camp, according to custom, where we could only avoid the maddening persecution of the mosquitoes by thrusting our heads into the smoke of the fire: of the two evils semi-suffocation was infinitely the less.

On Monday morning we started at 4.30, and soon reached the first rapid, where the river narrows down to some thirty yards wide. A fall compelled us to make a portage of a quarter of a mile. After traversing a few miles of smooth water, we encountered in the next fifteen an unbroken series of heavy rapids, in one of which we narrowly escaped a disastrous accident, for our canoe became caught under a heavy fall as we were trying to haul her upstream. Luckily we managed to extricate it intact, and the only damage suffered was the loss of a few articles and a thorough drenching of the rest.

After some days of hard work we left the rapids behind, greatly to our relief, and emerged on to a large lake, which we crossed, only to encounter, to our disgust, rapids much more formidable than those we had just passed.

A Thousand Miles from a Post Office

The banks of the river at this point were still lined with ice, although it was the middle of July, an unwelcome addition to the difficulties and dangers of the rapids, and it was with the greatest delight that we came at length to the broad expanse of a large lake, which the Indians called Sucholintoa. This lake divides the head-waters of the Tha-anni from those of the Fish River. From the top of a neighbouring hill, some five hundred feet high, we obtained a magnificent view of the surrounding country.

It was possible to trace the courses of the two rivers almost down to the coast, and never before had I seen such a network of lakes and streams as was spread out beneath my eyes on that occasion. The country was wild and desolate in appearance, and almost treeless. Traces of an Eskimo encampment were visible, but no signs of the natives themselves.

From this lake we proceeded by a small river through another smaller lake into a large lake, which the Indians called Thaolintoa or Pipestone Lake, from the shores of which the Eskimos and Indians obtain the soft pipestone used in manufacturing pipes, stone lamps, and cooking utensils.

This lake is fully twenty miles in length, running east and west, and about half that distance in breadth. Deer abounded in the vicinity, and we had no difficulty in keeping ourselves well supplied with all the fresh meat we needed. At the western end of this lake we entered the Upper Tha-anni River, a fine broad stream with very swift current but no rapids, which took us into Tha-anni Lake, a magnificent sheet of water over sixty miles in length, though divided into three parts by narrow channels. The first part, nearly twenty miles long, is bounded on the north by bare, bleak hills, of no great height, and on the south by lower land studded with a few stunted pine-trees. Here we came upon traces of Indians, of no recent date, however, being probably two or three years old. Heavy ice greatly impeded our progress and several times compelled us to make portages over its surface. On entering the third section of the lake we altered our course so as to strike the north-west corner, where the Indians often camp in the autumn. The aspect of the country remained unchanged, bare, bleak, and treeless.

Although we were now within three days' journey of Lake Yath Kiad, or Yathkyed, on the Kazan River (visited in the year 1894 by Mr. J. B. Tyrrell and his party), the reported dwelling-place of large numbers of Eskimos, we nevertheless resolved to retrace our steps, not thinking it wise to penetrate farther into the desolate interior, especially as we had seen no traces of recent encampments and the time we had allowed for the trip was up.

On the 23rd of July, therefore, we started for home, after having explored a deep bay in which we found a number of old tents abandoned by their owners in the previous summer. With a fair wind we sailed across the lake until the ice put an end to that easy mode of travelling. The wind was still in our favour when we re-entered the river, and by its aid, together with the swift current, we covered the distance to Lake Thaolintoa in thirteen hours. It had taken us four days to accomplish that much on the way up.

At Lake Thaolintoa we decided to return by way of the Fish River. A succession of short portages and paddles across small lakes brought us to Lake Todatara, from which we soon reached the river. The current was very swift, but there was fortunately an absence of rapids until we had descended its course to within 20 miles of the coast. In shooting these we nearly came to grief more than once: at length, however, we arrived at the coast in safety, and were not a little surprised to find that the return trip had taken only half the time we had spent in ascending the Tha-anni.

We were very fortunate in getting fine weather during our trip along the coast, and reached Churchill on the last day of July, after an absence of only twenty-five days. Our early return caused considerable astonishment, for the Indians at the post had predicted that we should be at least six weeks on the journey. The trip had been undertaken with the object of locating the Eskimos and Indians of the interior, and to investigate the feasibility of establishing a Mission amongst them. I append

FIG. 3. TOURBIÈRE IN SUMMER SHOWING PANS.

a short extract from a report I sent in to the Bishop of Moosonee on my return:

" It is fully proved that the Eskimos and Indians of these regions and those much farther north can be reached by the Tha-anni or Fish Rivers in three weeks from Churchill, but the great difficulty would be in taking in supplies to maintain a man or men at this outpost. It would be no feather-bed missionary work, and would require a man willing to put up with the hardest life possible."

No effort in this direction has been made up to the present, nor do I see any probability of any being attempted in the near future. We must be content to minister to these people on their irregular visits to Churchill, our most northerly station, described in 1895 by Bishop Newnham as " the dumping off place . . . end of the world . t'other side of nowhere."

Since the above was written there is a prospect of the establishment of a mission station at Chesterfield Inlet, where a very large number of Eskimos are to be met with, but the Chipewyan Indians do not go so far into the north country.

CHAPTER XXII

INFLUENCE OF MISSION WORK ON THE INDIAN CHARACTER

ON my return from the north the work of the Mission amongst the Eskimos and Indians was renewed with increased vigour as the results of our efforts became more and more apparent year by year. The mollifying influence it seemed to exert over the sullen Indian character was especially gratifying.

When we first came to Churchill we found their superstitions and apathy most discouraging. In striking contrast to the Eskimos, who are exceed. ingly grateful for the least thing done for them, the Indians were entirely different, a people, it seemed, to whom gratitude was unknown: in fact, as I have already mentioned, the term "Thank you" does not exist in the Chipewyan language, neither did it seem to exist in their thoughts. If you gave them anything, they would snatch it out of your hand and hide it away as if afraid you might change your mind. Towards their women they were callous and inconsiderate to a degree, treating them as beasts of burden, hewers of wood and drawers of water. In days gone by a man would scorn to help his wife to erect the tent, cut firewood, or carry a burden of any kind—this was women's work. Laden with naught but his gun he stalked on ahead whilst his wife trudged along behind, bent under a heavy load with possibly one or two children on top.

Shortly after reaching Churchill I gathered the men together in church and had a long and severe talk with them on this matter. Indian-like they listened and smiled, but for a long time would say nothing; then one of the oldest men amongst them got up and said, as only an Indian can say, " They had listened to the *Yalti* (minister) and knew that what he said was right and true, but their forefathers had always acted in this way and they could not change." On one occasion I passed through some Indian tents on my way to church, with my wife leaning on my arm. To our surprise we saw the Indians watching us very closely, evidently highly amused at the very strange spectacle of a man assisting his wife, a thing they would have scorned to do. But, thank God, we lived to see all this changed. I well remember one young fellow who helped his sick wife to church for many weeks, even carrying her across creeks and swamps on his back or in his arms, and in church finding her places in the service books and tending her with unremitting care. It became a common sight to see an Indian man thus helping his wife and occasionally even carrying the baby. No longer was the aged and infirm father or mother left to die alone in the wilds according to the ancient custom. I have known Indians to haul their old and sick people for days together, nursing them with the greatest tenderness on the way. Anyone who has a practical and not a mere theoretical knowledge of Indian life in the far north will understand what this means, and what testimony it bears to the wonderful power of the Gospel. I have seen the time when I could understand and even sympathize with the Indians leaving their sick and aged to die.

After the mild excitement occasioned by the arrival and departure of the annual ship had subsided we settled down to the winter's work. The strain was beginning to tell on both my wife and myself, and we were forced to recognize the fact that we could not stand the strenuous life of the north very much longer; especially was this the case with my wife, who, since the birth of our one child, had never been so strong as formerly.

However, in the following April I paid my usual visit to York Factory in order to give the Indians of the district an opportunity of partaking of Holy Communion and to baptize any children who might have been born since my last visit. It is really wonderful how much these people reverence the Sacraments: no hardship is so severe, no distance so great, as to cause them to forego an opportunity of obtaining them. Some people, of course, might say, " Oh yes, this is all superstition; they look upon these things as a sort of fetish;" if so, I can only wish we had more of this sort of fetish amongst civilized Christians.

As a case in point, I remember that whilst on a visit to York Factory one Easter, Joseph Kitche-kesik, our native catechist, tramped in from Severn, 275 miles away, all alone, and dependent entirely upon his gun for support. To my rather angry remonstrance (for I feared that he would be unable to return to his post until the summer) he very calmly replied: "For eighteen months I have had no opportunity of kneeling at the Lord's Table: I knew you would be here for Easter: therefore I came."

After spending Easter Day with us he started back alone, as he had come, hauling his flat sled, which carried his blankets and a few pounds of food.

Prevented by the fast-melting snow from returning through the woods, he struck right out along the shores of the Bay, where the ice was still firm. At night, however, he was unable to reach the shore owing to a large stream of water betwixt him and the coast, formed by the melting snow. Unable to get ashore to camp in the woods, he was compelled to wrap himself in his robe and sleep on the ice without either shelter or fire. He made a meal of biscuit washed down by a drink of ice water, for he could not, of course, cook anything, and spent the night alone on the ice several miles from the shore. A second night was spent in a similar manner, and on the third day he managed to get ashore and gain the shelter of the woods, through which he tramped until he reached his destination at the end of the tenth day, having travelled 550 miles to partake of Holy Communion with me at York. Devotion such as this seems to put to shame the perfunctory zeal of many civilized Christians, apparently proving that in too many instances the Sacraments are esteemed in proportion to the difficulty experienced in obtaining them. There is such a thing as making the Gospel too cheap.

On my way home from this visit at York, which lasted about a week, we encountered such very severe weather—the thermometer being far below zero—that my face and legs were very badly frozen. The severity and duration of the winter on the shores of the Bay may be readily imagined from the fact that the date of my return was the 19th of April, within two weeks of the beginning of May. I was completely used up and fain to confess that I could not stand the life much longer: a younger man was needed for it.

A week or two later, however, I was off again to visit some Indians at Seal River, 30 miles north of Churchill. For fifteen hours, from 5 a.m. to 8 p.m., we tramped on, frequently having to wade through water which lay nearly a foot deep on the ice. After a stay of only a day or two we set out to return, and found this journey much more trying than the going, for we were in water up to the knees nearly all the way, and in several places it rose to our waists, and the dogs had to swim. We reached home in an exhausted state after twenty hours of this sort of travelling.

These expeditions are of a nature sufficiently arduous to take a great deal out of any man; and though at the time their exhausting effects are merely general and temporary, it is impossible for anyone to undertake them year after year without impairing the strongest constitution. At first I seemed able to stand any amount of hardship: no amount of exposure seemed to affect me, and I was accustomed to sleeping on the wet—not merely damp—ground without the slightest fear or uneasiness. Now, however, I could no longer do so in spite of the heartfelt joy experienced in ministering to the poor souls starving spiritually, and often physically, in the desolate wilderness of the north.

CHAPTER XXIII

A LONG AND TEDIOUS JOURNEY HOME TO ENGLAND
(1898)

DURING the early summer things so turned out that we had to decide to give up our work. Our departure was to take place as soon as the annual ship arrived from England, for, although we were not sailing for home by the Hudson's Bay vessel—as I had to return by way of Winnipeg in order to visit York, and if possible Split Lake—yet we had to wait for the ship so as to obtain a passage in the coast-boats which were to carry the portion of her cargo intended for York, as the captain had refused to go to that port on account of the difficulty of getting into the harbour there.

The ship arrived on the 6th of August, and on the 10th we were told to be in readiness to embark on the boats next morning.

The people amongst whom we had laboured so long, Chipewyans, Eskimos, and English-speaking natives, greatly affected by the approaching loss of their pastor, implored me to remain with them and I had quite decided to stick to my post for some time longer, and let my wife go home in the ship, when a serious illness of my wife in July forced me to alter my resolution.

It was impossible to send her home alone as intended, for she was still confined to her bed when the ship arrived. She was so weak on the 10th that she had to be carried down to the boats. Many of our people had assembled at the landing to see us off, and there were few dry eyes amongst them when we bade them a final adieu. Taking our places in the boats, we proceeded 5 miles down the river to where the *Eric* was at anchor, and, by the kind courtesy of the captain, were permitted to spend the night on board, which was much more comfortable than the boat. She was to tow us out of the river in the early morning.

Soon after 3 a.m. the officer in charge of the boats roused us out in a great hurry, insisting that we must start at once as the wind was fair, and without so much as a cup of tea which the captain wanted to get for us, we were bundled into the boats. My wife had to be carried into the boat we were to occupy. It was full of all kinds of cargo, and the only accommodation at our disposal was a small cabin, 6 feet square, ventilated solely by its narrow door. For six days and nights Mrs. Lofthouse, in no condition to withstand the unpleasant motion of a small boat, lay on the floor of this tiny cabin wrapped in a rabbit-skin robe. During the whole of that time she was unable to take any food, and when we reached York was so weak that she could neither stand nor walk.

A Thousand Miles from a Post Office

A week's stay here greatly benefited her health, though she was hardly in a fit condition to undertake a canoe trip of 400 miles: there was, however, no other course open to us but to continue our journey in faith and hope. The York Indians greatly appreciated our brief sojourn in their midst, and we spent a very happy week in ministering to their needs.

The weather had been very unsettled for some days, but the morning of the 24th, the day of our departure, dawned clear and fine, a happy omen and answer to the prayers of many friends. Our party of seven embarked in two canoes already almost filled with baggage and provisions. In the first, paddled by two York Indians, were my wife and I. The second contained our faithful Joseph Kitchekesik, a native girl, and an Indian boy. We were all packed very much after the manner of the proverbial herrings and sardines.

Camp was pitched on the first evening a few miles up the Hayes River. In spite of the short distance traversed, we were only too glad to have an opportunity of stretching our cramped limbs: the dampness of the ground was a minor evil.

The weather continued to be favourable, and we made excellent progress each day; nevertheless, it was somewhat trying to sit still for fourteen or sixteen hours every day, and especially so for my wife, so that our day of rest on Sunday came as a welcome relief. A quiet day in camp, with two enjoyable services in which our Indians took part,

172

afforded us a chance to recoup our energies and relieved the monotony of the journey.

During the greater part of the week following we were working up rapids and making long portages, for there are nearly forty portages between York and Oxford House in coming up the river. Among many uncomfortable days and nights that of the 3rd of September was, without doubt, the most wretched.

The day had been very hot, heavy thunderstorms had passed over us, and the long paddle across Knee Lake had tired the men very much Consequently, when we encountered a rather lengthy and formidable rapid late in the evening, we resolved to pitch our tents as soon as we had carried our outfit to the head of the cataract. It proved to be a very bad place for a camp, but as the storm seemed over, and we were very tired, we thought it would do for the short night. In a slight hollow in the rocks, therefore, the only place available, our tent was pitched and weighted down with stones, as it was impossible to make use of tent pegs, and after supper and prayers we turned in to a well-earned rest as we thought. About an hour later a terrific storm burst upon us: a violent gale beat full against the door of our tent, and rain fell in torrents. As I was lying on the most exposed side of the tent, I was the first to become aware that the water was simply pouring in and saturating our blankets and rabbitskin robe. Almost immediately we found ourselves standing in 3 inches of water, and were obliged to hang on to the tent poles to prevent it from being blown into the river, only a few yards away. In this altitude we were forced to remain throughout the whole night, for though the rain ceased after some hours the gale continued with unabated vigour, and we had to sit up the whole night

At dawn the men departed in search of firewood, and after several attempts succeeded in starting a fire. Fortified by a cup of tea, we stood for some time around the fire in an endeavour to keep warm, a wretched-looking group in sodden garments, for it still continued to rain, though not so heavily as it had done. Finally we resolved to push on to Oxford House, which was only half a day's journey away. Three or four portages had to be made before we reached there; the trails were through high willows, so that when we reached the post we looked and felt like half-drowned rats.

Two days' rest was required to reinvigorate our exhausted bodies and to dry our saturated clothing. On few occasions have I appreciated shelter, warm food, dry clothing, and a bed so much as at that time.

Leaving Oxford, a journey of six days brought us to Norway House, where we arrived without incident on the thirty-second day from leaving our home at Churchill. On the following day we were agreeably surprised by the arrival of a Mr. C. Chapman, a young layman from Canada, who was on his way to continue our work at Churchill. His advent greatly cheered me, for I was beginning to be despondent and fearful lest the discontinuance of the work at Churchill should cause a return to faithlessness and barbarism amongst the flock we had left. It was my earnest wish to return with him, for I knew better than he, or any other man, the trials of the lonely life to which he was devoting himself. My wife would not, however, hear of this for a moment. No doubt she was in a better position than I to judge of my fitness to undertake the journey. As we were now in the land of steamers I was able to leave my wife to continue the journey to Winnipeg alone, whilst I was free at any rate to accompany Mr. Chapman as far as Split Lake, beyond which I had promised faithfully I would not go.

With our native catechist and the two York Indians, we descended the Nelson River for 260 miles to Split Lake, passing Cross Lake on our way.

This river is one of the most difficult and dangerous streams in the north to canoe upon; many of its rapids are very bad, and it is full of whirlpools in certain places. Mr. Chapman, who had spent many years in the Muskoka country, and had often run rapids before, considered himself an expert canoeman, but after running an exceptionally dangerous rapid, where he wisely followed my advice and sat still in the bottom of the canoe, remarked to me, with a very white face, " Mr. Lofthouse, if there are any more rapids like that on the river, let us get out and walk." I reassured him by saying that the Indians would never attempt an impossible rapid, and that when left to themselves, and not interfered with by white men, their skill and care was such that accidents were almost unknown.

We reached Split Lake in five days, and there we parted, he to go on with two Indians to York Factory via Fox Lake and River, I to rejoin my wife in Winnipeg. By a curious coincidence Mr. Chapman reached York on the 2nd of October, the very date of my arrival there fourteen years previously.

A pleasant stay of a few days at Split Lake enabled me to appreciate the excellent work done by our native catechist, and then I set out to return to Norway House, which I reached on the 3rd of October.

Soon afterwards I started to cross Lake Winnipeg in a small York boat, as the last steamer of the season had already left. On the 15th of October, after a most stormy voyage in cold and snowy weather, we landed at Selkirk, twenty miles from Winnipeg, and my canoe journeying of over two months' duration was at an end.

The last stage, however, of five or six thousand miles by land and sea still remained, but we were now in the midst of the luxuries of modern travel. There would be no more days of uncomfortable canoeing, no more rapids, no wading of icy rivers, and no nights of hunger and exposure.

A Long and Tedious Journey to England

It is difficult for me even at this distance of time to conceal a smile when I hear fellow-travellers in Pullman cars and ocean liners complain loudly at some trifling inconvenience or disturbance. I always wish they could spend a few months with me in the north; when they returned there would be no more grumbling—at least, for a time.

From Winnipeg we made our way to New York via Montreal, and on the 15th of December landed in Liverpool after four months of continuous travelling since leaving our little home in the north—" the last house in the world," as it has been well called.

CHAPTER XXIV

ANOTHER VENTURE IN THE NORTH
(1899)

AFTER I had spent some six months in England, doing deputation work for the Church Missionary Society and raising some funds for our own Missions in the Hudson's Bay country, Bishop Newnham wrote me urging, if possible, my return to the Diocese to establish our Mission of Split Lake, as he had secured a man for that work, and wished me to go with him and spend some months there.

It was quite impossible for my wife and family to accompany me, so I arranged for them to remain in England, and in July I returned to Canada as Archdeacon of Keewatin, an honour which I had refused when the Bishop was in the north in 1895.

In passing through Eastern Canada I stayed for a few days with my old friend Mr. J. W. Tyrrell in Hamilton, and was informed that the Canadian Government was planning an expedition to explore and survey the Barren Lands of the north from Edmonton to Marble Island on Hudson's Bay, and that Mr. Tyrrell had been asked to undertake this. He was very anxious that I should accompany him as one of his staff. This I was very willing to do, if I could get the consent of my Bishop, for it would give me the very opportunity I had wanted for years of reaching the more northerly of our Eskimos. I therefore wrote the Bishop, who happened to be in Canada, and he willingly gave his consent. Mr. Tyrrell got me appointed, and I arranged to meet him in Winnipeg the following December, when the expedition was to start.

Going on to Winnipeg I met Bishop Newnham in August. He was again about to visit the Missions in the north, and had secured a young student from St. John's College, named Fox, to go to Split Lake, and I was to accompany him, spend some months with him, and then return to Winnipeg to meet Mr. Tyrrell and start for the northland.

Mr. Fox was ordained in Winnipeg, and in August we all started across Lake Winnipeg, Bishop Newnham taking with him Mrs. Chapman and her two children to join her husband at Churchill. Our two parties kept together until we reached the Nelson River some twenty miles north of Norway House, when Bishop Newnham and his party took the usual canoe route to York Factory, which I had so often followed, whilst Mr. Fox and I went down the Nelson River to Split Lake.

The weather was not too kind to us, for it rained constantly, but rain or no rain we had to travel, and Mr. Fox, new to the country and the mode of travel, found it, as all new-comers do, rather trying to sit all day in an open canoe with the rain pouring down upon him. We had one specially bad time the day after we left Norway House, and Mr. Fox told me afterwards that had we been within reach of a steamer he would certainly have turned back. Fortunately we were in a place where turning back was impossible, for Mr. Fox afterwards proved himself one of the very best missionaries we ever had in the north, and put in some fifteen years of most devoted service. He got a remarkable hold of the Cree language, in which he could both think, speak, and even dream.

We reached Split Lake without anything worse than soaked clothing, and took up our abode in a very small and not quite watertight lean-to room, in which few people in England would have kept their cattle; but there was no other to be had, so we had to be content.

Our first work was to construct a mission house, and at this we both worked much more than eight hours a day, our recreation being holding services with the Indians in a small log shack which had been built for the catechist, there being as yet no church.

As soon as the winter set in, which was early in November, I began visiting the Indians in the surrounding country, often travelling 50 miles a day on my snow-shoes. There were about seventy-five families or roughly three hundred souls scattered over hundreds of miles of country. In this way the time passed very quickly, and the last week in November I started on my tramp of 500 miles to

Another Venture in the North

Winnipeg. On the 1st of December I reached Norway House, 250 miles away, where we rested for two or three days, and I greatly enjoyed the comfort of a bed and decent meals at the Methodist mission station where Dr. Mason had first laboured before he joined the Church of England and began work at York Factory.

Leaving Norway House we tramped round the north end of Lake Winnipeg up the Saskatchewan River at Grand Rapids, then across Cedar Lake into Winnipegosis until we struck the railway at a place called Mossy, and in a few hours I was back in Winnipeg none the worse for another three months of a very rough life.

Upon reaching Winnipeg I found that our expedition had been delayed. I therefore went down to Eastern Canada to spend Christmas, a railway journey of near three thousand miles there and back !

Early in February, 1900, our party, or rather part of it, met in Winnipeg and from there went on to Edmonton, where we completed our party of nine and made final arrangements for our trip of ten months.

It was, however, the 15th of the month before we could make a start. The first part was a run of 150 miles by horse-teams, which is a very luxurious method of travel compared with plodding on snow-shoes. We reached Lac-la-Bêche in comfort, and there got our four dog-teams and started out for a walk of 1,150 miles. This was not done in a day or so, but meant keeping on for two months until we got on the edge of the Barren Lands. Here we had to wait until the ice cleared out of the lakes and we could take to our canoes. It is quite impossible in this present volume to give any idea of this journey, but I may do so at some future time.

We were away from Edmonton just ten months, travelled 5,000 miles by snow-shoes and canoe, never slept in a bed, or met with any of the camp comforts to be found in Africa or more genial climes.

We got back to Winnipeg on the 15th of December, and on the 18th I started for England and reached my home and family just too late for Christmas. In going over my notes I found that I had travelled over twenty thousand miles in eighteen months, and that nearly six thousand of this was on snow-shoes or by canoe.

After staying four months in England I again started for Canada in order to go down to Moose Factory, where I first landed in 1882, to take charge of the work there during Bishop Newnham's absence in England. Going on to Missinābie on the Canadian Pacific Railway, I took to my canoe and travelled down the same river up which I came in 1883, before the C.P.R. was completed.

This trip is really a very pleasant one, being only a matter of some six days. There are some rather heavy rapids, but none of them are at all dangerous. I had with me a young clergyman going to begin his work as a missionary at Rupert's House, and we arrived about the end of May. There had been but few changes since I first landed nearly twenty years before, for changes come slowly in this part of the world.

During the winter I visited Albany, 100 miles north of Moose, and Rupert's House, 60 miles south, both of which are flourishing mission stations. Both of these trips were really picnics compared to most of the journeys in the north, as I was enabled to travel in comfort, riding behind a good team of dogs.

It was a busy but happy time, and the winter and spring passed very pleasantly, and early in June Bishop Newnham and his family arrived bringing the, to me, surprising news that in the previous April I had been appointed the first Bishop of Keewatin, a diocese formed from the north-western portion of Moosonee and a large part of the Diocese of Rupert's Land.

Leaving Moose about the middle of June, I therefore made my way back to Missinabie and so on to Winnipeg, where I spent the whole of July in visiting many of the places in the new diocese, and on the 17th of August I was consecrated Bishop of Keewatin.

Thus my first twenty years of work in the north was ended, to be followed by eighteen years of quite as strenuous work and travel elsewhere, until I had to resign in December, 1920. It was with much pain and sorrow that I gave up my work; but during the last four years of that period I lost both my wife and

A Thousand Miles from a Post Office

only daughter, and my own health was beginning to give way under the strain.

My wife's death was due entirely to the twelve years of real suffering and privation so bravely endured on the shores of that vast inland sea where Henry Hudson, the discoverer, whose grave remains unknown even to this day, laid down his life.

PRINTED IN GREAT BRITAIN BY
BILLING AND SONS, LTD., GUILDFORD AND ESHER

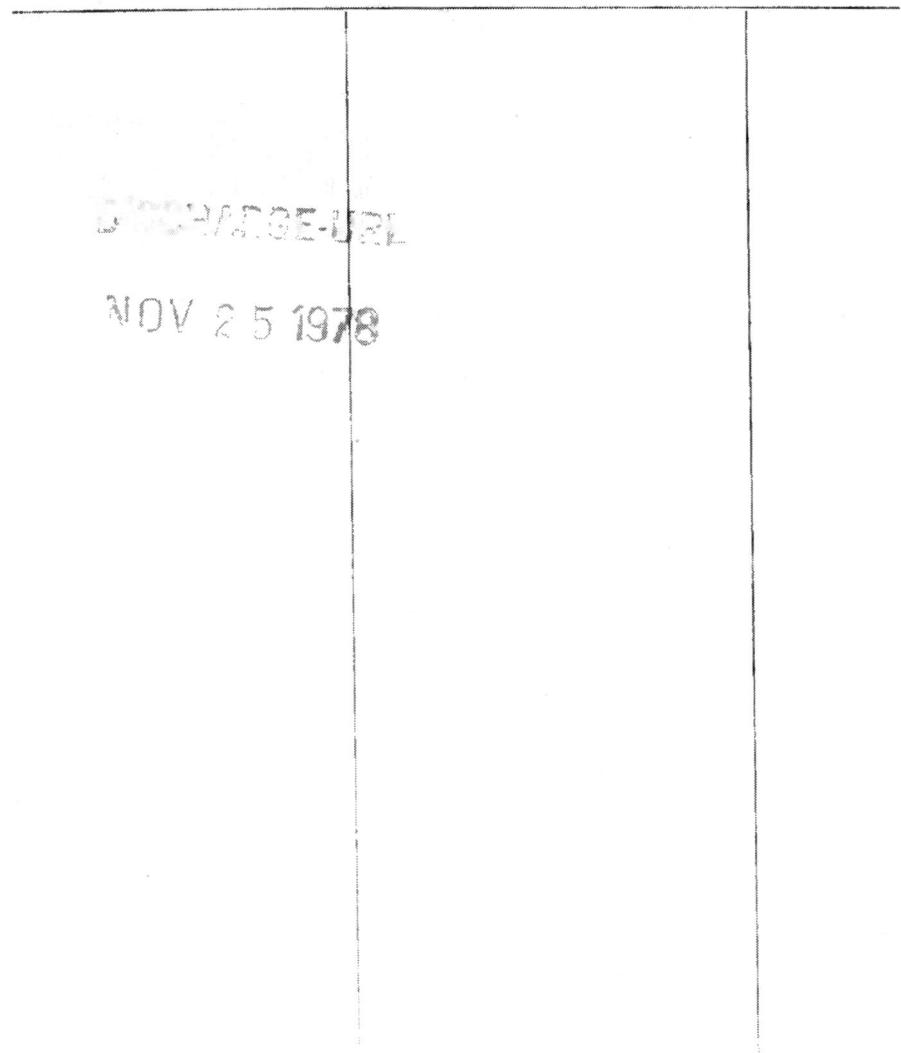

ImTheStory.com

Lightning Source UK Ltd.
Milton Keynes UK
UKOW02f1126231214

243593UK00021B/1315/P